LAUGHTER
Still Is
THE BEST MEDICINE

LAUGHTER
Still Is
THE BEST MEDICINE

OUR MOST HILARIOUS JOKES,
GAGS, AND CARTOONS

Reader's Digest

The Reader's Digest Association, Inc.
New York, NY/Montreal

A READER'S DIGEST BOOK

Copyright ©2014 The Reader's Digest Association, Inc.
All rights reserved. Unauthorized reproduction, in any manner, is prohibited.
Reader's Digest and Laughter, the Best Medicine are registered trademarks of
The Reader's Digest Association, Inc.

Library of Congress Cataloging-in-Publication Data
Laughter still is the best medicine : our most hilarious jokes, gags, and cartoons /
editors of Reader's Digest.
    pages cm
 Summary: "The editors of Reader's Digest present over a 1000 of our all-time
favorite jokes, gags and cartoons from the humor pages of our magazine. This
hilarious collection offers up some of the funniest moments that get us through
our day, in the form of jokes, gags and cartoons that will have readers laughing out
loud"-- Provided by publisher.
 ISBN 978-1-62145-137-2 (hardback) -- ISBN 978-1-62145-148-8 (epub)
1. American wit and humor. I. Reader's Digest Association.
PN6165.L377 2013
808.87--dc23
                               2013024092

Cover design and spot illustrations: George McKeon
Project Manager and Art Director: Elizabeth Tunnicliffe
Cartoon Credits: Ian Baker: *124, 204;* John Caldwell: *6, 61, 78, 108, 150, 160, 181;*
Dave Carpenter: *29, 96;* Roy Delgado: *44, 86, 113, 169, 209;* Ralph Hagen: *32, 41, 69, 121,
173;* Mike Lynch: *93, 116;* Scott Arthur Masear: *11, 144, 147;* Harley Schwadron: *72, 136, 155;*
Steve Smeltzer: *24, 133;* Thomas Bros.: *14, 48, 64, 83, 103, 164, 176, 188, 193, 212;*
Kim Warp: *57;* Elizabeth Westley & Steven Mach: *19, 53, 129, 201*

We are committed to both the quality of our products and the service we provide
to our customers. We value your comments, so please feel free to contact us.

                    The Reader's Digest Association, Inc.
                    Adult Trade Publishing
                    44 S. Broadway
                    White Plains, NY 10601

For more Reader's Digest products and information, visit our website:

                    www.rd.com (in the United States)
                    www.readersdigest.ca (in Canada)

Printed in China

1 3 5 7 9 10 8 6 4 2

CONTENTS

A Note from the Editors

Have you ever stopped to consider just how unattractive laughter is? People are rarely at their best when caught mid-guffaw. Here, try this experiment. Walk over to someone and tell them a funny joke, say, the one on page 86. Now sit back and watch. Their eyes crinkle and their wrinkles become really pronounced. Their nostrils flare. Strange animal-like sounds escape from their mouths. Sometimes out of their noses. Occasionally out of their ears. They show a lot of teeth and gums. Sometimes they laugh so hard they spit out food or their eyes water. Who would enable such conduct?

We would!

We're not particularly attractive people here at *Reader's Digest,* so we consider humor the great equalizer. Besides, laughter is what we do best. We've been sharing jokes ever since the Goths invaded the Red Sox, or whoever they went after. We have a library full of hilarious jokes, cartoons, and one-liners, not to mention anecdotes about family, friends, work, and even military life. And this volume is filled with the best of them. So go ahead, take a read. But whatever you do, please don't laugh.

VENUS
and
MARS

"To be happy with a man you must understand him a lot and love him a little. To be happy with a woman you must love her a lot and not try to understand her at all."

—HELEN ROWLAND

COURTSHIP QUIPS

Ole and Inge were in their car heading for Minneapolis when Ole put his hand on Inge's knee.

"Ole," she murmured softly, "you can go further if you want." And so he drove to Duluth.

—DICK FLOERSHEIMER

Dating is complicated. You don't believe us?
Here are some examples:

- Right after we broke up, my ex-girlfriend called to ask how to change her relationship status on Facebook.

- I got into a 90-minute argument with my girlfriend because she was adamant that *Moby-Dick* was a true story. I finally let her win so I could go to sleep.

- My now ex-girlfriend and I were in my room one day, and the Internet was particularly slow. After I complained, she suggested that I untangle my Ethernet cord so that more Internet could get through.

- I recently joined an online dating site, and one of my matches was my first cousin.

An enormously wealthy 65-year-old man falls in love with a young woman in her 20s and is contemplating a proposal. "Do you think she'd marry me if I tell her I'm 45?" he asked his friend.

"Your chances are better," said the friend, **"if you tell her you're 90."**

—PROSANTA CHAKRABARTY

" If he likes *you* better, how come he always
buys *me* perfume?!**"**

My girlfriend and I worry about different things.
One day, I was like, "What do you fear the most?"
And she was like, "I fear you'll meet someone else,
and you'll leave me, and I'll be all alone."
And she was like, "What do you fear the most?"

And I was like, "Bears."

—COMEDIAN MIKE BIRBIGLIA

"Why doesn't your mother like me?" a woman asks her boyfriend.

"Don't take it personally," he assures her. "She's never liked anyone I've dated. I once dated someone exactly like her, and that didn't work out at all."

"What happened?"

"My father couldn't stand her."

—JAMES RICHENS

Driving my friend Steve and his girlfriend to the airport, we passed a billboard showing a bikini-clad beauty holding a can of beer. Steve's girlfriend glanced up at it and announced, "I suppose if I drank a six-pack of that brand, I'd look like her."

"No," Steve corrected. "If *I* drank a six-pack, you'd look like her."

—JOHN D. BOYD

Visiting the *Musée Marmottan Monet* in Paris, I was awestruck by one of Monet's water lily paintings. I whispered to my boyfriend that I would happily give everything I owned for the huge, stunning painting. Ever practical, he whispered, "And it still wouldn't be enough."

—REBECCA TRUMAN

Last winter I was laid up at home with the flu. My fiancée called and volunteered to come over, fix dinner and play nursemaid to me. I declined, not wanting to pass on the flu to her.

"Okay, honey," she told me. "We'll wait till after we get married. Then we'll spend the rest of our lives making each other sick!"

—STEVE POMERANTZ

A couple is lying in bed one night when the woman turns to the man, smiles and says, "I'm going to make you the happiest man in the world."

The man replies, "I'll miss you."

BLISSFUL BANTER

When I ran out of shampoo, I borrowed some from my wife. Later, I complained that the scent was too feminine for my taste.

"No problem," she said. "Just dab a little gasoline behind each ear. You'll smell fine."

—PIERRE LAPLANTE

A married couple has been out shopping for hours when the wife realizes that her husband has disappeared. So she calls his cell phone.

"Where are you?!" she yells.

"Darling," he says, "do you remember that jewelry shop, the one where you saw that diamond necklace you loved? But I didn't have enough money at the time, so I said, 'Baby, it'll be yours one day'?"

"Yes!" she shouts excitedly.

"Well, I'm in the bar next door."

—BONNIE TOWNSEND

Thomas Bros.

" I guess you have another excuse not to take out the garbage. "

On a business trip to New Orleans, my son-in-law Mike bought a set of expensive kitchen knives for his wife. His coworker was surprised.

"You shouldn't buy such an expensive gift for your wife on a business trip," he said. "She'll think you've been up to something."

"If I'd been up to something," Mike replied, "I wouldn't be bringing her knives."

—LINDA BRUMLEY

My wife got pulled over for making an "S" turn. She started to make a "U," then changed her mind.

—COMEDIAN GABE ABELSON

Overheard at my garden-club meeting: "I never knew what compost was until I met my husband."

—MARY HALLER

I was nervous the first time my husband and I were hired to photograph a wedding. Making matters worse, we arrived at the wrong venue. In a panic, we bolted out of the building—my husband in the lead and me trailing behind, in tears. As we fled, I heard a security guard remark, "That ceremony didn't go too well."

—JOANNE CAMPBELL

After learning that her parents were in a minor car accident, my wife called her mother.

"What happened?" she asked.

"I was driving and fell asleep," said her mother, irritated. "And of course, your father wasn't paying attention!"

—GUY LAMBERT

For some reason the bookstore clerk couldn't get the computer to recognize my preferred customer card. Peering over her shoulder at the screen, I said, "There's part of the problem. It shows my birth date as 12/31/1899."

"That's right," my husband chimed in. "She was born in June, not December."

—M. PATRICIA CAPIN

My grandmother figured that breakfast time was as good a time as any to get something off her chest. So over morning coffee, she turned to my grandfather and said, "We've been married 56 years, and it still seems that you are always correcting me."

Grandpa replied, "We've been married 58 years."

—CALEB ZELLERS

Leena was tired of her husband coming home drunk and decided to scare him straight. One night, she put on a devil costume and hid behind a tree to intercept him on the way home. When her husband walked by, she jumped out and stood before him with her red horns, long tail, and pitchfork.

"Who are you?" he slurred.

"I'm the devil," she answered.

"Well, come on home with me," he said. "I married your sister."

My dapper 51-year-old husband supervises scads of attractive younger women at his law firm. After friends divorced, I had to ask. "Honey, have you ever been tempted by the idea of a May-December romance?"

"Not really," he replied. "I don't see myself dating older women."

—SUSAN FERGUSON

Suspecting he had a serious medical condition, I nagged my husband until he agreed to see a doctor. Once there, he was handed a mountain of forms to fill out. Next to "Reason for visit?" he wrote, "My wife made me."

—SUSAN HUTTON

I came down with the flu and wanted my husband to do some of the housecleaning. I wasn't sure how to tell him, so I tried reverse psychology.

"Honey, I'm sorry I'm leaving you with such a mess," I said between sniffles. "The laundry needs to be done, the dishes washed, the floors cleaned."

"Don't you worry," he said sympathetically. "It can all wait until you feel up to it."

—GAIL WHITE

One friend complained to another, "All my husband and I do anymore is fight. I've been so upset, I've lost 20 pounds."

"If it's that bad, why don't you just leave him?" asked the second friend.

"I'd like to lose another 15 pounds first."

—MARY BUOYE

In the natural childbirth classes my wife and I took, the birthing process was represented by a hand puppet being pushed through a sock. So at the actual birth, I was shocked to see all this blood. The thing I had prepared myself for was a lot of lint.

—COMEDIAN STEVE SCROVAN

My husband will not be confused for Jamie Oliver anytime soon. Before I ran off to work, I gave him detailed instructions on how to cook dinner. That evening, I returned home to find a dry chicken roasting in the oven next to a Pyrex measuring cup full of water.

"What's that doing in there?" I asked.

Clearly offended, he sputtered, "You told me to put the chicken in the oven with a cup of water!"

—PAM BRENNAN

The garage called to say that the car we had taken in to be serviced was ready.

"Great," I said. "My wife's in the bathroom 'getting beautiful,' and we'll be over as soon as she's finished."

The voice on the other end asked, **"Will that be today?"**

—NORMAN JANSSEN

At the end of a crazy day, my husband and I collapsed on our bed and watched TV. As I made myself comfortable in the crook of his arm, I said, "Know what's comforting? When I'm old and gray, I can lean on you, and you'll still feel young and strong. Isn't that wonderful?"

"For you, maybe," he said. "I get the old, shriveled lady."

—LISA LIPMAN

While standing on an eight-foot ladder, trimming a bush that grew across the top of our garage door, I realized that if my wife entered the garage from the house and pushed the opener, it might spell doom for me. So I climbed down and, unable to find her, scribbled a note and stuck it to the opener: "Push Button and Kill Tom."

I finished my pruning job and went about my yard work. Later I went into the house, and my wife said, "I don't understand your note in the garage. I pushed the button, and the only thing that happened was that the garage door opened."

—TOM BROWN

My friend's wife came home to find her husband entrenched in front of the TV set, switching between a fishing show and an erotic movie. After a few minutes of back-and-forth, she offered this suggestion: "Honey, you might as well just watch the erotic movie. You already know how to fish."

—MARJORIE LONG

In the doghouse with my wife, I ordered her some flowers and told the florist that the card should read, "I'm sorry, I love you."

Unfortunately, my instructions must not have been clear enough. When the flowers arrived, the card read, "I'm sorry I love you."

—MARK S. MAURER

" It wasn't his fortune. I married him for his mind, but then that went too.**"**

My husband has always been disdainful of people who, in his estimation, talk too much. Recently he proudly told me he'd heard that men use 2200 words a day, while women use 4400.

I pondered that a moment, then concluded, "That's because women have to repeat everything they say to their husbands."

He looked up and asked, **"Come again?"**

—DARLENE KELLY

During birth-preparation class, we were learning relaxation techniques, and the instructor asked us to come up with ideas to lower stress levels. Silence pervaded the room, but one dad, a slight fellow with round glasses and a religious T-shirt, finally offered: "Prayer?"

"Good," the instructor replied. "Anything else?"

"How about sex?" suggested another father-to-be.

Once again, silence followed. Then the devout dad-to-be muttered under his breath, "What do you think I've been praying for?"

—TRACY AND SCOTT YANCEY

I was dining in our Georgia town, when a tourist stopped by my table.

"Excuse me," he said. "But my wife loves your sandals. Did you buy them locally?"

"Yes, just down the street," I said.

"May I ask how much they cost?"

"They were $77."

"Thank you." He then hollered to his wife, "Honey, she got them in Florida."

—REBA CRISP

During a recent vacation in Las Vegas, I went to see a popular magic show. After one especially amazing feat, a man from the back of the theater yelled, "How'd you do that?"

"I could tell you, sir," the magician answered. "But then I'd have to kill you."

After a short pause, the man yelled back, "Okay, then—just tell my wife!"

—SUZANNE OLIVER

My wife and I were going through a rough patch financially, but we kept ourselves sane by repeating, "As long as we have each other, we don't need anything else." But when the television and radio in our bedroom broke within a few days of each other, my wife lost it.

"That's just great!" she shouted. "Now there's no entertainment in our bedroom at all!"

—VINCENT DAY

While working for the Social Security Administration, I helped an elderly woman—who was no longer married—fill out her claim form.

Reading off a question, I asked, "How did your marriage end?"

"Just fine," she said, grinning a little too broadly. "He died."

—WILLIS BIRD

My husband and I were driving past our neighbors' home when I noticed a decorative wooden stork in their driveway.

"Did they have a baby?" I asked.

"I don't know," he said. "Why?"

"There's a stork in their yard."

"Dear," he said, "that's not the way it happens."

—JENNIFER WALKER

My husband asked me to dress up as a nurse tonight to fulfill his fantasy . . . **that we have health insurance.**

—COMEDIAN WENDY LIEBMAN

My wife and I were at the circus watching a shapely young woman dangling from a trapeze. The woman appeared to be wearing a very revealing costume, and my wife exclaimed, "There's nothing underneath!"

At first I agreed, but studying the woman closely, I saw there was flesh-colored material under her costume. So I said, "Yes, there's flesh-colored material underneath."

My wife replied, "I meant there is no net underneath the trapeze. What were you referring to?"

—THANE LAFOLLETTE

My wife asked me if I thought she looked fat in her new dress. Pointing to what I was wearing, I replied, "Do I look stupid in this shirt?"

—BRIAN RICE

A woman was having a passionate affair with an exterminator when her husband arrived home unexpectedly.

"Quick," she said to her lover, "into the closet!" And she pushed him into the closet, stark naked.

The husband, however, became suspicious. And after looking high and low, he discovered the man in the closet.

"Who are you?" he demanded.

"I'm an exterminator," said the man.

"What are you doing in there?"

"I'm investigating a complaint about an infestation of moths."

"And where are your clothes?"

The man looked down at himself and cried, "Those little bums!"

QUOTABLE QUOTES

"AS SOON AS WOMEN START REGISTERING A COMPLAINT, MEN CALL IT NAGGING."

—STEVE HARVEY

"I have bad luck with women. A woman I was dating told me on the phone, 'I have to go. There's a telemarketer on the other line.'"

—ZACH GALIFIANAKIS

"IF LOVE IS THE ANSWER, COULD YOU REPHRASE THE QUESTION?"

—LILY TOMLIN

"We all want to be in love and find that person who is going to love us no matter how our feet smell, no matter how angry we get one day, no matter the things we say that we don't mean."

—WILL SMITH

"I love being married. It's so great to find that one special person you want to annoy for the rest of your life."

—RITA RUDNER

"A MARRIED MAN SHOULD FORGET HIS MISTAKES; NO USE TWO PEOPLE REMEMBERING THE SAME THING."

—DUANE DEWEL

"Marriage has no guarantees. If that's what you're looking for, go live with a car battery."

—ERMA BOMBECK

"If there hadn't been women, we'd still be squatting in a cave eating raw meat, because we made civilization in order to impress our girlfriends."

—ORSON WELLES

"I've been told that when you meet the right person, you know immediately. How come when you meet the wrong person, it takes a year and a half?"

—COMEDIAN PHIL HANLEY

"I can handle my wife's *Honey-Do* list.
It's her *Honey-Don't* list that just about kills me."

My ex-husband was both difficult and prescient. Before our wedding, I declared in a fit of pique, "John, I don't know if I should marry you or leave you."

John replied, "Well, baby, you'll probably do both."

—JANET STREET

Bob went over to his friend Joe's house and was amazed at how well Joe treated his wife. He often told her how attractive she was, complimented her on her cooking and showered her with hugs and kisses.

"Geez," Bob remarked later, "you really make a big fuss over your wife."

"I started to appreciate her more about six months ago," Joe said. "It has revived our marriage, and we couldn't be happier."

Inspired, Bob hurried home, hugged his wife, told her how much he loved her and said he wanted to hear all about her day. But she burst into tears. "Honey," Bob said, "what's the matter?"

"This has been the worst day," she replied. "This morning Billy fell off his bike and hurt his ankle, then the washing machine broke. Now, to top it off, you come home drunk!"

—LYNDELL LEATHERMAN

My parents divorced when I was two but remained friends. So much so that on my wedding day, Dad toasted my husband and me by saying, "I hope y'all are as happy together as your mother and I are apart."

—MELANIE FRANKLIN

How many divorced men does it take to change a lightbulb?

Who cares? They never get the house anyway.

ELSPETH MCVIE

During a heartfelt chat with her friend about relationships, my wife sighed and said, "You know, if something happened to Lloyd, I don't think I could ever marry again."

Her friend nodded sympathetically.

"I know what you mean," she said. "Once is enough."

—LLOYD G. YOUNG

With a new baby and a new car, my husband and I realized that we wouldn't have any extra money to buy each other gifts for our first anniversary. We decided to wait a few months and buy gifts on the anniversary of the day we met.

My husband seemed pleased with the idea. He then pulled a piece of paper out of his pocket. "The first anniversary is supposed to be paper," he confessed, "but I didn't think you'd be too happy with this."

I unfolded the paper. Inside he had scribbled a little heart with the letters I.O.U.

—TIFFANY BEHRENS

Because my husband and I were having trouble conceiving, we paid regular visits to a fertility clinic. One day, Andy's parents were over. The clinic called while I was out and left detailed instructions on our answering machine for what to do in bed later that night. I relayed the message to Andy.

"Yeah, I know," he said. "I had the messages playing and went to the bathroom. When I came out, Dad told me."

—CRYSTAL HOUGHTON

Shortly after I married, my parents came to visit. To please my father I made a buttermilk pie, a treat I know he liked but rarely got to eat.

After everyone proclaimed it delicious, my father smiled nostalgically and said, "Susan, do you know you're only the second person ever to make buttermilk pie for me?"

Because my mother is not known for her baking, I was surprised by this comment. "Mom," I asked, "did you make him a buttermilk pie?"

"Of course!" she replied.

Dad thought for a second and said, "Then I guess you're the third."

—SUSAN E. ANDREWS

A friend parked his car at the supermarket and was walking past an empty cart when a woman asked, "Excuse me, sir, did you want that shopping cart?"

"No, I don't," he answered. "I'm only after one thing."

As he walked toward the store, he heard her murmur, "Typical male."

—ABBY MECHLING

While I was attending church, someone yelled out my husband's name. It was his long-lost cousin, whom he hadn't seen in 40 years.

"It's amazing that you could recognize him after all this time," I marveled.

"Yes," said his wife. **"He was always good at remembering useless things."**

—MARGARET BOWMAN

WRINKLE CREAM

After one glance at my updated driver's license photo, I said the first thing that came to mind: "Ugghhh!"

"What's wrong?" the DMV clerk asked.

"I look ancient in this picture."

"Well, look at the bright side: In five years, you'll love it."

—ANDREA RAITER

When you're young and you get to choose between sleep and sex, you take sex every time. You start getting older, you get to choose between sleep and sex, you choose sleep and just hope you have a dream about sex.

—JEFF FOXWORTHY

We'd finally built our dream home, but the contractor had a concern: the placement of an atrium window for our walk-in shower. "I'm afraid your neighbors might have a good view of you au naturel," he said.

My middle-aged wife put him at ease. "Don't worry," she said. "They'll only look once."

—GREGG BARNER

At a senior citizens' function, I watched an older fellow ease his wife ahead of him in line. "You ask for the tickets, dear," he told her. "You look older than I do."

Seeming to ignore his uncomplimentary remark, she stepped up to the counter. "I'd like two tickets, please," she said loudly. **"One for me, and one for my father."**

—JEAN L. SCHAUER

I knew I was going bald **because it was taking longer and longer to wash my face.**

—COMEDIAN HARRY HILL

On my 40th birthday, I waltzed out of my bedroom dressed in an old outfit.

"I wore this on my 30th birthday. I guess that means my wardrobe is ten years old," I said to my husband, hoping he'd take the hint and buy me some clothes as a present.

"Or," he offered instead, "it means when you were 30, you had the body of a 40-year-old."

—BETH GEFFERS

I was taking my 50th birthday pretty well until I went to visit my family. I have two aunts living in different nursing homes.

When I visited Aunt Alice, she blurted out, "Jennifer, you are getting gray."

"Well, yes," I admitted. "But I still feel young."

I put the thought aside until I drove over to see my other aunt. "You look so young and healthy," my aunt Bernice gushed. "How do you do it? You have a youthful glow."

I thanked her for the compliment but couldn't resist telling her about Aunt Alice's comment on my gray hair.

"Well, yes, it's true," Aunt Bernice acknowledged. "Alice was always blessed with better eyesight than I."

—JENNIFER CUMMINGS

My grandma always says that she never gets any phone calls. So for her birthday, I put one of those "How's my driving?" bumper stickers on her car. The phone's pretty much ringing off the hook now.

—COMEDIAN CHRIS HOBBS

While visiting a retirement community, my wife and I decided to do some shopping and soon became separated. "Excuse me," I said, approaching a clerk. "I'm looking for my wife. She has white hair and is wearing white shoes." Gesturing around the store, the clerk responded, "Take your pick."

—ALBERT CUTINI

Three old friends are taking a memory test. The doctor asks the first, "What's three times three?"

"Two hundred seventy-four," he answers.

"Hm." The doctor turns to the second man. "What's three times three?"

"Tuesday," he replies.

"What's three times three?" the doc asks the last man.

"Nine," he answers.

"Great," the doctor says. "How did you get that?"

"Simple. I subtracted 274 from Tuesday."

—AMIT RASTOGI

No longer relishing my reputation as a technophobe, I bought an iPhone and peppered the young salesman with a ton of questions.

"Please excuse my ignorance," I said. "I'm from the Smith-Corona generation." He had no clue what I was talking about, so I asked, "Do you know what a Smith-Corona is?"

He replied tentatively, "A drink?"

—VICTORIA GEIBEL

After imbibing at her young son's birthday party, an angry Tina Gonzales bit her Naples, Florida, neighbor. Cops pinned the crime on her by counting tooth marks on the victim. Gonzales was the only adult present with all her teeth.

❝ I'm middle-aged, thirty pounds overweight and balding. Quite frankly, I couldn't think of anything scarier than that. ❞

When my husband returned from a jog, I joked, "What are you running from?"

"Old age," he said.

"Oh, yeah? Then what are those gray hairs on your head?"

"Camouflage."

—ANN HANSEN

• • • • • • • • • • • • • • •

An old man was rowing a boat on a lake when a frog swam up to him and yelled, "Mister! Mister! I'm really a beautiful princess. Kiss me and we'll live happily ever after!" The man put the frog in his pocket and rowed to shore. The frog called out again, "Hey, mister! I'm really a gorgeous princess. Kiss me, and we'll live happily ever after!"

Still the man said nothing and walked down the road toward town. The frog was getting angry at being ignored. "Why don't you kiss me? I told you I'm really a beautiful princess."

"Listen, lady," the man replied. "I'm 90 years old. At this point in my life I'd rather have a talking frog."

—CHANTELL WILLIAMS

Two guys are sitting in a bar when one of them casually points to a couple of old drunks sitting across from them and says, "That's us in ten years."

His friend disagrees. "That's a mirror."

—TESS ELLIOTT

As my dad approached his 40th birthday, he visited the Department of Motor Vehicles to renew his driver's license. A lifeguard in his youth, Dad is particularly proud of his once-blond hair, which has darkened considerably over the years. Still, under "hair color" on the application, he wrote "blond."

As the DMV clerk reviewed the form, she muttered to herself, "Eyes: blue; Hair: brown," at which point Dad interrupted politely with, "Excuse me, my hair is blond."

The woman looked up and, without skipping a beat, told him, "Yes, sir. But here we call that shade of blond brown."

—BETH VAN BRUSSEL

I overheard two EMT volunteers talking about the time they went to the aid of an elderly man. As one took down his information, the other opened his shirt to attach EKG cables. "Any history of heart trouble?" asked the first volunteer. "None," said the patient. Looking at the telltale scars of bypass surgery, the second volunteer wasn't so sure. "In that case," he said, "do you remember when the lion attacked you?"

—MONICA GILLIGAN

Our group was third in line behind two other foursomes at the golf course. A young man in the first group walloped his tee shot straight down the middle of the 410-yard fairway to within a few yards of the green.

"Wow," said an older man in the second foursome, "I don't even go that far on vacation."

—RICHARD C. PETERS

I called a patient to confirm an appointment with the doctor I work for, and her husband answered.

"Hello, may I speak with Anna?"

"Who?" he said.

"Anna."

"Santa?"

"No, Anna."

"Who is this?"

"This is the doctor's office calling for Anna."

"Who?"

"The doctor's office calling for Anna!"

"Oh, Anna," he said. "You better talk to me; Anna's hard of hearing."

—D.P.

My college roommate and I have remained good friends, and now that we're hitting middle age, I never miss a chance to kid him about being older than I am—even if it's only by one month. So for his 40th birthday I gave him a not-so-subtle jab by gift-wrapping a CD by the British reggae group UB40.

A month later, he sent me my own birthday gift—the latest release from the Irish rock band U2.

—JOHN DAVIS

My nine-year-old daughter walked in while I was getting ready for work.

"What are you doing?" she asked.

"Putting on my wrinkle cream," I answered.

"Oh," she said, walking away. "I thought they were natural."

—DEB FILLMAN

You could have knocked me over with a feather when my two older daughters, both in their 50s, announced they were marrying their long-time boyfriends.

"Well, no one can accuse them of having a shotgun wedding," I joked when I shared the good news with their younger sister.

"You got that right," Lori agreed. "More like a stun gun wedding."

—DOROTHY AMATO

Recently I sat in a restaurant watching two older men go at it. It quickly grew heated as one of them declared, **"I'm so mad, I'm taking you off my pallbearer list!"**

—TOM CALVERT

After church one Sunday, my wife, Norma, and I went out for lunch. Outside the restaurant, a schoolmate I hadn't seen for 50 years recognized me, and we stopped to chat while my wife went ahead into the restaurant.

"Wow!" I said when I joined Norma, "that guy told me I haven't changed since Grade 9."

Norma laughed. "You mean," she said, "you looked that old when you were in Grade 9?"

—WOLF MAYDELL

You know you are no longer a kid when:

- Driving a car doesn't always sound like fun.

- You laugh at your parents' jokes.

- You don't buy a new sports car because of the insurance premiums.

- You actually buy scarves, gloves and sunscreen.

- You leave ballgames early to beat the crowd.

- The only thing in your cereal box is cereal.

- You look into the surveillance-camera monitor at a convenience store and wonder who the overweight guy with the bald spot is, then realize that it's a shot of you from behind.

—LYNDELL LEATHERMAN

A woman walked up to a little old man rocking in a chair on his porch. "I couldn't help notice how happy you look," she said. "What's your secret for a long and happy life?"

"I smoke three packs of cigarettes a day," he said. "I also drink a case of whiskey a week, eat fatty foods and never exercise."

"That's amazing," the woman said. "How old are you?"

"Twenty-six."

• • • • • • • • • • • • • • • •

Our family was at an outdoor fair watching a caricature artist at work, when a 50-something woman stopped to watch as well. When she saw that the artist charged $15 for a color caricature, she gasped, "Fifteen dollars—just to have someone draw my wrinkles!"

The artist turned slowly and studied her face for a moment before replying, "I don't see any wrinkles."

She immediately sat down and had her portrait drawn.

—MARGARET WELLS

A new patient reported to his doctor and asked: "Doctor, do you think I'll live to be a ripe old age?"

The doctor asked: "Are you married?"

The patient said he wasn't.

"Do you smoke?"

"No."

"Do you drink?"

Again the patient answered in the negative.

"Do you follow a healthy diet?"

"Very healthy, Doctor."

"Have you ever been in hospital for treatment?" continued the doctor.

"Never."

"Do you ever go out on the town and not get home until dawn?"

"Never. I wouldn't do anything like that."

"Are there many women in your life?" asked the doctor.

"Not a one," admitted the patient.

"Well," concluded the doctor, "you probably will live to be a ripe old age. But I wonder if it'll be worth it."

—MARTIEN STASSEN

BATTLE OF THE BULGE

Needing to shed a few pounds, my husband and I went on a diet that had specific recipes for each meal of the day. I followed the recipes closely, dividing each in half for our individual plates. We felt terrific and thought the diet was wonderful—we never felt hungry!

But then we realized we were gaining weight, not losing it, and I checked the recipes again. There, in fine print, was: "Serves 6."

—BARBARA CURRIE

After peering at myself in the mirror, I looked dolefully at my husband and complained, "I'm fat."

Responding with the tact, sympathy, and carefully chosen words that I've come to expect, he said, "I'm fat too."

—BETH HARTZELL

My friend Kimberly announced that she had started a diet to lose some pounds she had put on recently.

"Good!" I exclaimed. "I'm ready to start a diet too. We can be dieting buddies and help each other out. When I feel the urge to drive out and get a burger and fries, I'll call you first."

"Great!" she replied. "I'll ride with you."

—KATINA FISHER

During a trip to the mall, my wife noticed the video store was having a clearance sale. Thinking she might find an exercise tape, she searched and searched but found nothing. Finally she asked a clerk where they might be.

"Exercise videos? They're located between Science Fiction and Horror," he said with a completely straight face.

—DALE MATSUDA

As I quizzed my driver's-education students about road signs, the one for Slow Moving Vehicle stumped them. So I offered them a hint by lifting the sign above my head and slowly parading up and down the room.

One student thought he had it: "Wide load!" he called out.

—VERN PINNT

The trouble with jogging is that by the time you realize you're not in shape for it, it's too far to walk back.

—FRANKLIN P. JONES

I was walking to lunch with my friend Tristan and discussing the need to start an exercise program. A mutual friend Chris joined us on the walk, and after listening to Tristan and I talk about fitness, Chris said, "I'm exercising every day."

"You're exercising?" we asked. "Daily?"

"Yeah!" he replied. "I swim after work on Mondays, Wednesdays and Fridays. And I run on Tuesdays and Thursdays."

We stopped walking, and I asked Chris, "How long have you been doing this?"

"Oh, I don't start until next week!" he replied.

—JAKE PEDROSA

The professor's last patient for the day asks: "Tell me, doctor, what is the best exercise to lose weight?"

"I advise you to move your head first to the right, then to the left. And how many times?"

"Every time someone offers you something to eat."

—KOMSOMOLSKAYA PRAVDA

Everyone is on this low-fat craze now. **The Mayo Clinic just changed its name to the Balsamic Vinaigrette Clinic.**

—BUZZ NUTLEY

Recently, I bought a step counter for my evening walks and soon began wearing it everywhere. While visiting my parents, I went for a walk with my mother, who noticed the counter on my belt.

"What's that?" she asked.

"An exercise tool," I replied. "It keeps track of your steps. It's to help you stay healthy and lose weight."

She gave me a quizzical look and said, "Don't you think it would work better if it counted your bites?"

—ANGELA GIACCI

An elderly patient paid me a wonderful compliment. "You're beautiful," she said.

I must have looked skeptical because she was quick to assure me that she was sincere. "It's just that I rarely hear flattering comments about my looks," I explained.

She smiled understandingly. "That's because you're fat. But it doesn't mean you aren't pretty."

—AMY MOTZ

My parents had one of those old-time rotary telephones. This drove my brother crazy. Once, he misdialed a long-distance number and had to do it all over again.

"Mom," he asked in frustration, "why don't you replace this thing with a touch-tone phone?"

"If we did," my mother said, "your father would never get any exercise."

—DEBRA COPELAND

" If I get dizzy and pass out, there's a cherry
danish in my lunch box. **"**

I was reading the nutrition labels on some cans of food when something caught my eye.

"What's saturated fat?" I asked my mother.

She answered, "Your father taking a shower."

—TOSHIA MITCHELL

The woman sashays out of the bedroom modeling a lovely garment.

"Look at this!" she says to her husband. "I've had it for 20 years, and it still fits."

Her husband nods. **"It's a scarf."**

—D. GOLIGHTLY

My husband was going on a diet, but when we pulled into a fast-food restaurant he ordered a milkshake. I pointed out that a shake isn't exactly the best snack for someone who wants to lose weight. He agreed but didn't change his order.

The long line must have given him time to make the connection between his order and his waistline. As the woman handed him his shake, she said, "Sorry about the wait."

"That's okay," he replied self-consciously. "I'm going to lose it."

—KAREN NAZARENUS

With fire alarms blaring at my mom's apartment complex, she grabbed her favorite bathing suit and ran out.

"A bathing suit?" I said later. "Of all the priceless things in that apartment, that's what you chose to save?"

"Material things come and go," she said. "But a one-piece suit that doesn't make you look fat is impossible to replace."

—CATHY PEACOCK

We put our old NordicTrack on the curb with a sign that read "Free: Fun exercise machine!" By that afternoon, it was gone. But the next day, it reappeared with this note attached: "Define fun."

A woman in our diet club was lamenting that she had gained weight. She'd made her family's favorite cake over the weekend, she reported, and they'd eaten half of it at dinner.

The next day, she said, she kept staring at the other half, until finally she cut a thin slice for herself. One slice led to another, and soon the whole cake was gone. The woman went on to tell us how upset she was with her lack of willpower and how she knew her husband would be disappointed.

Everyone commiserated, until someone asked what her husband said when he found out. She smiled. "He never found out. I made another cake and ate half!"

—BARBARA A. JOSLIN

My sister's dieting stint ended the day her eight-year-old saw the price tag on her weight-loss shake.
"Whoa!" he yelled out.

"Eight bucks for this, and it doesn't even work."

—D.W.

On my husband's second visit to the exercise class he enrolled in, he used the rowing machines, rode a stationary bicycle and did leg exercises with one-kilo weights attached to each ankle. When he finished, he walked ten minutes to the garage where he had parked his car, then picked me up.

"I'm exhausted," he complained. "I wonder if I should continue this program."

When we got home, he trudged into the house and finally sat down to rest his tired legs. He eased his shoes off—and discovered the weights still strapped to his ankles.

—RENATE HUXTABLE

For several years, I had been trying to convince my husband that he should do more cardiovascular exercise. One day, he announced that he was going golfing at our local course and that he was going to walk instead of riding in a cart.

I thought this was a good start to getting in shape and that my nagging was finally paying off. When he came back, he walked into the house moaning and groaning over how much his back and his legs hurt.

"What does that tell you?" I asked.

He replied, "It tells me I should have taken the cart!"

—MAGGIE WHEELER

" I've lost 80 pounds, and nobody notices it. "

Scientists are now saying that obesity can be caused by viruses. **I guess you have to eat a lot of them.**

—GREGG SIEGEL

The teacher in our Bible class asked a woman to read from the Book of Numbers about the Israelites wandering in the desert.

"The Lord heard you when you wailed, 'If only we had meat to eat!'" she began. "Now the Lord will give you meat. You will not eat it for just one day, or two days, or five, or ten or twenty days, but for a month—until you loathe it."

When the woman finished, she paused, looked up and said, "Hey, isn't that the Atkins diet?"

—DAVID MARTINO

Clearly I was not going to win the battle of the bulge on my own, so I decided to join a gym.

"Before you start working out, we like to do a health assessment," explained the gym representative. "When you come in, wear loose-fitting clothing."

"If I had loose-fitting clothing, we wouldn't be having this conversation."

—KELLY BLACKWELL

My friend's husband asked her what she'd like for her 40th birthday.

"Oh, something that will make me look beautiful and feel good," she said.

Hoping for an expensive new outfit or a trip to a spa, she was surprised but excited on her birthday morning when he left a large box waiting for her in the hallway.

Inside it was an exercise bike.

—JENNY GRAHAM

Did you hear about the sword-swallower who was on a diet?

He was on pins and needles for six weeks.

— TODD S. HARRIS

A note on the soda machine in our break room warned, "Diet cola isn't working."

Beneath that, someone else had written, "Try exercise and a low-carb diet."

—PAUL COOPER

Early one Saturday, I checked out a local yard sale and came across some exercise equipment I had been looking for. As I paid the owner for her Thighmaster and aerobic step, I inquired if she also had a Buttmaster.

"No," she replied quickly, "but I should have it in time for my next yard sale."

—MELODY LEAR

My husband and I were standing in line at the Pittsburgh airport ticket counter. The wait got the best of me, and I left him holding our place while I looked for a seat. There were no chairs around, so I settled on a substitute—an opening in the counter where suitcases are pushed through to the ticket agents.

As I sat there, I noticed several people smiling at me. I became a little self-conscious when I saw a few of them nudge others to look in my direction. I squirmed around uncomfortably—and that's when I noticed the screen above my head flashing my weight in green lights every time I wiggled.

—JAN LARKEY

FAMILY FUN

"I never met anyone who didn't have a very smart child. What happens to these children, you wonder, when they reach adulthood?"

—FRAN LEBOWITZ

" Oh my God, we forgot the kids. "

PARENTING PRIDE

At the airport, Sylvia was anxiously waiting for her daughter's plane. After graduating from college, Ashley had been gone a year, adventuring in faraway places. Sylvia's heart raced when she saw her lovely child step out of the Jetway. Then she noticed a tall man directly behind Ashley, dressed in feathers and beads, with exotic markings all over his body. Ashley greeted her mother and introduced the man as her husband. Sylvia felt faint. She screamed, "I said you should marry a rich doctor! A rich doctor!"

—CHRIS PARKE

Having found her daughter playing doctor with the neighbor's son, the irate mother marched across the street to confront his parents.

"Oh, don't take it so seriously," the kid's mother said. "It's only natural for children their age to want to satisfy their curiosity."

"Curiosity? Curiosity?" the girl's mother said, fuming. "He removed her appendix!"

I realized my family didn't get out enough when we went to a restaurant recently: We had just finished eating when my five-year-old brother got up from the table and headed for the kitchen, dishes in hand.

—ANTHONY PRYOR

As a new parent, I've come to appreciate the sacrifices my mother and father made for me. For example, not long ago, I thanked my mother for all the time and money that was spent on me for orthodontics.

"We had to," she said, "or you would still be living at home."

—KRIS BOEDIGHEIMER

Overheard:

Mom: You're 18. You can do what you want.
Daughter: So I can run away!?
Mom: No. You're 18. You would just be leaving.
Daughter: Oh.

—LAURA MORRISON

On his 18th birthday, my son announced that he was no longer obligated to observe the curfew we'd imposed on him.

"I'm 18," he announced. "And you can't stop me from leaving the house if and when I want to."

"You're right," I said. "I can't stop you from leaving. But I can stop you from coming back."

—PAUL ENNIS

When I took my ten-year-old grandson to his first flea market, I taught him the fine art of haggling.

"Say someone's selling a hunting knife for $20. Offer him $15," I instructed. He got the concept, and when he spotted a ring he wanted that was selling for $5, he went into action.

"I only have $3," he told the woman at the booth.

She smiled. "Then $3 it is."

With that, he pulled out a $5 bill and waited for change.

—CINDY COLEMAN

My parents, married 45 years, raised a brood of 11 children. Now they enjoy 22 grandchildren. When asked the secret for staying together all that time, my mother replies, "Many years ago we made a promise to each other: **The first one to pack up and leave has to take all the kids.**"

—BETTY STUMPF

At the supermarket, a rambunctious child stopped moving long enough to stare at my neck brace.

"What happened to her?" he asked his mother.

Seeing a great teaching opportunity, she replied, "Maybe she wasn't sitting down in her grocery cart!"

—HARRYL HOLLINGSWORTH

During a church social activity, I had to say a few words about myself. I mentioned that I was born in Quebec, that the first Côté had immigrated in 1635, and that I was a tenth-generation Canadian.

"I doubt anybody in this room can beat that," I boasted.

"I can!" came a voice from the back. Everyone turned around. It was my daughter.

—ALAIN CÔTÉ

To celebrate her parents' Golden Wedding anniversary, their daughter gave them two tickets to a lavish performance of classical ballet. It was the first time they had been to the opera. The next day, the daughter asked them for their impressions.

"Oh! It was wonderful," her father replied. "They were so graceful and kind. When they saw your mother asleep in her seat, they danced on tip-toe not to wake her up."

—EVELYN KATZ

I was thrilled to be moving into my own house, even though it was only a block away from my parents'. The first morning on my own I relaxed on the porch and listened to some music, enjoying my new independence.

Then the phone rang. It was my father telling me to turn the sound system down.

—ELI STICKLER

Spotted on a bumper sticker:
"I'm not a brat. Am not, am not, am not!"

—JACQUELINE PORTER

After discussing my dating life—or lack thereof—with my mother, I told her about a friend of mine who had been in a terrible car accident, broken both her legs, and wound up marrying her orthopedic surgeon. My mother sighed: "Why can't anything like that ever happen to you?"

—BARBARA ALBRIGHT

I had never been so zonked in my life. After my first child, Amanda, was born, my mother came to stay with me for a few weeks to help out, but I still woke up whenever the baby made the slightest sound during the night. One morning, I groggily asked my mom, "How long before I stop hearing every noise Amanda makes?"

Mom was obviously only half-listening. "Honey, are you coming down with something?" she asked. "You were coughing in your sleep."

—CAROL HERLONG

A mother is waiting for her son excitedly on the last day of term.

"At last you're home. Where's your report?"

"I haven't got it."

"How come?"

"I lent it to Béla."

"And why does he need it?"

"He wants to scare his parents with it."

—GYULA MECSÉRI

"I'm not sure Mary's ready for motherhood."

One day the four-year-old boy I babysit told me he was going to have a baby sister. Knowing that his parents wanted more children, I asked, "So when are you going to get this baby?"

"Daddy says as soon as I start sleeping in my own bed," was his innocent reply.

—HILLARY GEORGE

As my mother headed out her office door last election day, she announced, "Well, I'm off to the polls to cancel my daughter's vote."

"You know," replied a colleague, "it doesn't matter how old they get. You still have to clean up behind them, don't you?"

—LAYNA REED

My husband and I drove a thousand miles with our three young children to visit my parents. The reunion included my two brothers' bustling families, plus other friends and relatives. As we were piling into our van for the return trip, my father offered us a fistful of bills "to help with gas."

"You don't have to pay us to come see you!" my husband said.

"We're not paying you to come," my mother quickly replied. "We're paying you to leave!"

—LYNDA SHENEFIELD

I am an anesthesiologist who frequently takes emergency calls. Late one evening, a teenage boy arrived in the operating room for an appendectomy, accompanied by his mother. He wore jeans and a T-shirt and had long, flowing hair. Prior to surgery, I asked if they had any questions.

Immediately the mother leaned over toward me. "Doctor," she whispered, "while you have him asleep, could you give him a haircut?"

—ERNST HEILBRUNN

I'd been secretly dating for several months, and it was time to break the news to my very protective father. My mother thought he'd take it better if she explained to him that my boyfriend was a marine who had just returned from Iraq. This pleased Dad immensely. **"A marine? Good!" he said. "That means he can take orders."**

—MELISSA ESMILLA

Listening to a speaker in church, I was impressed that he still recalled his father telling him to "remember who you are" before he left the house. I leaned over to my 18-year-old son and whispered, "Is there anything that I used to say to you that stands out in your mind?"

He pondered, then leaned over and whispered, "Bring back the change."

—LAURA CRAPO

While my parents were painting their bedroom, my five-year-old sister walked in and asked, "What the hell are you doing?" Not realizing what she had said, she casually walked out.

After she left, my stunned dad then turned to my mother and asked, "Where the hell did she learn to talk like that?"

—MARJORIE ERICKSON

My two daughters were discussing the less than desirable physical attributes they had inherited from their father.

The older one: "I hate my freckles from Dad."

Her unsympathetic younger sister: "At least you got his freckles. I got his eyebrow."

—TAMMY RIDDLE

While watching the Olympics, my mother turned to my sister and said, "You just know the athletes' mothers are so proud of them. I'm proud of you girls, and you're nothing."

—LESLIE MCCLURG

A woman calls her husband to tell him that their two sons want to go to the zoo, then a movie. "That's too expensive," he says. "It's one or the other." "Okay, which one do you prefer?"

"Mikey."

Two little boys, ages eight and ten, were always getting into trouble. The boys' mother heard that a preacher in town had been successful in disciplining children, so she asked if he would speak to them. The preacher agreed, but asked to see them individually.

The mother sent the eight-year-old in the morning. The preacher, a huge man with a deep booming voice, sat the younger boy down and asked him sternly, "Do you know where God is, son?"

The boy's mouth dropped open, but he made no response, sitting there wide-eyed with his mouth hanging open.

So the preacher repeated the question in an even sterner tone, "Where is God?!"

Again, the boy made no attempt to answer.

The preacher raised his voice even more and shook his finger in the boy's face and bellowed, "WHERE IS GOD?!"

The boy screamed and bolted out of the room, ran directly home and dove into his closet, slamming the door behind him.

When his older brother found him in the closet, he asked, "What happened?"

The younger brother, gasping for breath, replied, "We are in BIG trouble this time! GOD is missing, and they think WE did it!"

—M & M TEE

"How many times do I have to tell you to slouch?"

Out shopping, my friend Darin noticed a mother with three little girls and a baby. The woman's patience was wearing thin as all the girls called "Mama" while she tried to shop.

Finally, Darin heard her say, "I don't want to hear the word "Mama" for at least five minutes."

A few seconds went by, then one girl tugged on her mom's skirt and said, "Excuse me, miss."

—MARIEL RAECHAL

Upset over a newlywed squabble with my husband, I went to my parents' house to complain. Trying to console me, my dad said that men aren't like this all the time.

"Baloney," I said. "Men are good for only one thing!"

"Yes," my mother interjected, "but how often do you have to parallel park?"

—JENNIFER L. LEE

On his birthday, my husband was stuck driving our six rambunctious children around. As usual, they were yelling, punching and annoying one another. Joel finally had had enough. "Kids," he said over the din, "if you would behave and be kind to each other, that would be a very nice birthday present for me."

Our six-year-old shot back: "Too late, I already got you another present."

—GAYLE TROTTER

Even though I'm in my 30s, I still stop by my parents' house to mow their lawn. One afternoon, the kid next door was cutting his grass at the same time.

"It's punishment for skipping a day of school," he explained. "Why are you still doing your folks' yard?"

"Because I cut a class when I was your age," I said with a straight face.

I'm told he's had perfect attendance ever since.

—ROBERT THOMPSON

I knew my kids watched too much TV when my seven-year-old asked me to pick him up from school at 3 p.m./2 p.m. Central.

—JOANNE LEVI

QUOTABLE QUOTES

"BECAUSE OF THEIR SIZE, PARENTS MAY BE DIFFICULT TO DISCIPLINE PROPERLY."

—P. J. O'ROURKE

"It's great to be a godmother. She calls me 'god' for short."

—ELLEN DEGENERES

"Don't bother discussing sex with small children. They rarely have anything to add."

—FRAN LEBOWITZ

"My mom buys paper plates, 300 in a big plastic bag. We can take one, but the rule is that we have to put the twist tie back on the bag. I guess it's to keep them fresh. Nothing ruins my lunch more than a stale plate."

—COMEDIAN JORDAN BRADY

"WHEN I WAS A KID, WE HAD A QUICKSAND BOX IN OUR BACKYARD. I WAS AN ONLY CHILD, EVENTUALLY."

—STEVEN WRIGHT

"The other night I ate at a real nice family restaurant. Every table had an argument going."

—GEORGE CARLIN

"MY MOTHER COULD MAKE ANYBODY FEEL GUILTY. SHE USED TO GET LETTERS OF APOLOGY FROM PEOPLE SHE DIDN'T EVEN KNOW."

—JOAN RIVERS

"A Harvard Medical School study has determined that rectal thermometers are still the best way to tell a baby's temperature. Plus, it really teaches the baby who's boss."

—TINA FEY

KIDS SAY THE DARNDEST THINGS

When my husband was away at basic training, my four-year-old daughter and I stayed with my sister. Since my daughter already called me Mommy, she started calling her aunt Mom—the way her six-year-old cousin did. One day, someone called. I picked up the extension and overheard the person ask my daughter if her daddy was home.

She said, "No, he's in the army."

"Is your mom home?" he asked.

"Yes, but she's asleep with Uncle Danny."

—TONYA ALEISAWI

"Now, who can spell the word straight?" the third-grade teacher asked her students.

"S-T-R-A-I-G-H-T," answered a boy seated in the front row.

"Great job. And do you know what it means?"

"Without ice."

—VICTOR CONWAY

My five-year-old son was badgering us to get him an iPad. "My friend brought his to school, and I want one too," he insisted.

"Absolutely not," said my husband. "They're expensive and fragile. Besides, what would you even do with an iPad?"

Our son replied, "I'd put it over my eye and play pirates with my friends."

—JULIE R.

On the day of my father-in-law's funeral, our two-year-old son was appropriately somber—until he spied the coffin. "Oooh, Mama!" he shouted. "Look at that big suitcase!"

—HELEN BALDWIN

"I have to go directly to the corner? I thought there would be an appeals process."

After downing half a glass of milk, my ten-year-old son declared, "I am an optimist: The glass is half-empty!"

"Looking at the glass as half-empty is a sign of pessimism," I said.

He corrected me: **"Not if you don't like what's in it."**

—PRATIK PANDYA

My three-year-old daughter, Chantelle, begged me for a story about when she was born.

"Daddy brought Mommy to the hospital, and the doctor helped you to be born," I began. "When you came out, we both said, 'What is it?' And the doctor said, 'It's a girl!' "

"How did the doctor know I was a girl?" asked Chantelle.

"Well, when you were born, you came to us with no clothes on."

"Ahh," said Chantelle. "And boys have clothes on."

—ANNETTE CAMPBELL

Usually, the secretary at my son's elementary school answers when I call, but on one occasion, I spoke to an unfamiliar voice.

"Do you know who it might have been?" I asked my son.

"It could have been Mrs. Campbell," he said thoughtfully. "Did it sound like she was wearing a blue coat?"

—MANDY WILLIAMS

My grandson is making great strides with his potty training, but every now and then, he waits too long before going. Once, sensing an emergency, he rushed into the bathroom—which was occupied by his mother—and shouted, "Scoot over!"

—CAROLYN WHITAKER

My six-year-old grandson watches a lot of TV. This became apparent the day he asked his father, "Am I healthy enough for sexual activity?"

—JOHN BALL

For our 20-year-old daughter's birthday, my wife gave her a laptop computer. When Lorena opened her gift and saw what it was, she reached for a tissue, saying, "Wait, I have something in my eye."

We all burst out laughing when her ten-year-old sister said, "It's called a tear."

—CLAUDE BÉCHARD

My two daughters were having a discussion about family resemblance. "I look like Mom," said my nine-year-old, "but I have Dad's eyes and Dad's lips."

The six-year-old said, "And I look just like Dad, but I have light hair." Then she turned to me. "Mom," she asked, "what does Dad have to do with us being born anyway?"

Her older sister jumped right in. "Don't be stupid, Christina. Dad is the one who drove Mom to the hospital."

—KATHLEEN O'NEILL

Scene: My son speaking to his three-year-old son.

Dad: Do you want to know a secret?
Son: Uh huh.
Dad: I love you.
Son: Do you want to know a secret?
Dad: Uh huh.
Son: I'm Batman.

—GARY PANKOW

"My dad said I should get the best education money can buy, so how much for an A?"

Three boys are boasting about their grandfathers.

"My grandpa is a great swimmer," says the first. "He can swim for hours!"

"That's nothing," says the second. "My grandpa goes swimming at six in the morning every day and doesn't get out till six at night."

"Big deal!" smirks the third boy. "My grandpa started swimming in this pond 20 years ago, and he still hasn't come out!"

While reviewing math symbols with my students, I drew a greater-than (>) and a less-than (<) sign on the whiteboard.

"Does anyone know what these mean?" I asked.

A boy raised his hand: "One means fast-forward, and the other means rewind."

—PEGGY HORACHEK

Our tour guide at historical Arlington National Cemetery thought he had an answer for everything . . . until he met our students.

"Excuse me," said one kid. "Are the graves in alphabetical order?"

—WILLIAM CULLEM

My six-year-old son, Michael, was so afraid of monsters lurking in his closet that he refused to go to bed. So I devised a plan to put his mind at ease: I filled a spray bottle with scented water and glued on a label that read "Creature Repellent."

This worked great . . . for a week.

"Monsters aren't real," I said, frustrated. "They're imaginary."

"Oh, yeah?" he shot back. "So how come they sell creature repellent?"

—ANNE-MARIE GIONET

An hour after I'd put my seven-year-old son to bed, I heard him cry out. I ran to his room, where I found him sobbing. "Mommy, I had a bad nightmare about a big monster," he said.

"And he had a face just like yours."

—DOROTHY AMARAL

Two letters arrived from my nine-year-old daughter, who was away at camp. One was addressed to Mom, the other to Dad. The sweet, short note to me said, "Dear Mom, I am having a lot of fun at camp. Tell Eddie [our cat] I miss him. I miss you. Love, Kenna." The even shorter note she sent to her father: "Dear Dad, Read Mom's note. Love, Kenna."

—ROBIN HOLT

When a teacher asked my six-year-old nephew why his handwriting wasn't as neat as usual, he responded, "I'm trying a new font."

—JUDITH FISHER

I asked my eighth graders, "Why are you looking forward to becoming a teenager?"
A student answered, "You're treated more like an adult because you are getting closer to adultery."

—KELLY THOMPSON

I gave an apple to a girl in our after-school program. It must have been very fresh, because she declared, "Mmm, I must get the recipe for this."

—LAURA MELVILLE

My young children had plenty of questions after witnessing a cat give birth. But I was ready. I grabbed a book off the shelf that explained in terms kids could understand how mommies and daddies have babies, one that I'd bought for this very occasion. But after I read it aloud, my four-year-old still wasn't satisfied.

"I don't want to know how people have babies," he said. "I want to know how cats have babies."

—FLORENCE MARCUS

During a fire drill at our child-care center, I asked the kids, "What would you do if I accidentally started a fire on the stove and your lunch was burning?"

One five-year-old knew: "I wouldn't eat that lunch."

—KAREN KIEFFER

My four-year-old grandson asked his mom why she couldn't drive him to day care. She said, "I have to breast-feed your little sister."

"Why can't Grandma do it?" he asked.

His mother explained that Grandma didn't have any milk.

"Then what's she got in there?" he asked. "Juice or something?"

—KIMBERLEY HOPPER

A young girl walked into her school library and asked the librarian—my daughter—for a particular book.

"Are you sure you want this book?" my daughter asked. "It's pretty scary."

"I'm not afraid of anything," said the girl. **"I've seen my grandmother naked."**

—ALFRED K. HARWELL

I was stepping out of the shower when my four-year-old daughter burst through the bathroom door.

"Excuse me!" I said. "I'm naked."

She responded, "Don't worry, I won't laugh at you."

—KODIE DAVIS

The teacher announced that to practice spelling, each member of the class would say what their father did for a living and then spell the occupation.

Mary went first. "My Dad is a baker, b-a-k-e-r, and if he were here, he would give everyone a cookie."

Next came Tommy. "My dad is a banker, b-a-n-k-e-r, and if he were here, he'd give each of us a quarter."

Third came Jimmy. "My dad is an electrician." But after struggling through a number of attempts to spell the word, the teacher asked him to sit and think about it for a moment while she called on someone else. She then turned to little Johnny.

"My dad is a bookie, b-o-o-k-i-e," Johnny said. "And if he were here, he'd lay you 8-to-5 that Jimmy ain't never gonna spell electrician."

—AL JENSEN

When my eight-year-old asked how I knew I was pregnant, I told her I had taken a pregnancy test.

"Oh," she said. "What questions were on the test?"

—LAUREL FALVO

I asked my three-year-old what she liked to eat.

"Nuts," she replied.

"Great," I said. "What kind? Pecans? Walnuts? Peanuts?"

"Donuts."

—B.L.

" My mom said I have to go to school if I want a house and a car, but frankly I don't think I'm ready for that much financial responsibility! **"**

My husband, a deputy district attorney, was teaching an antidrug class to a group of Cub Scouts. When he asked if anyone could list the gateway drugs, one Scout had the answer: "Cigarettes, beer and marinara."

—LORI WOLF

When my seven-year-old daughter was diagnosed with diabetes, a new diet regimen was called for.

"Do you think you could eat green beans?" I asked.

"No," she said. "I haven't liked green beans since the accident."

"What accident?"

"When I accidentally ate a green bean."

—MINDY KROPF

My five-year-old nephew has always happily answered to BJ. That ended when he came home from his first day of school in a foul mood. It seems his teacher took roll, and he never heard his name.

"Why didn't anyone tell me my name was William?!" he complained.

—GREG CLAUSER

A salesman rang the bell at a suburban home, and the door was opened by a nine-year-old boy puffing on a long black cigar. Hiding his amazement, the salesman asked the young man, "Is your mother home?"

The boy took the cigar out of his mouth, flicked ashes on the carpet and asked, "What do you think?"

—JONATHAN DINGLER

The topic for my third-grade class was genetics. Smiling broadly, I pointed to my dimples and asked, "What trait do you think I passed on to my children?"

One student called out, "Wrinkles!"

—LYNN GRAGG

While cleaning our bathroom, I noticed some spots on the wall next to the sink. I scrubbed the stains but didn't make much progress. Puzzled, I asked my son if he knew anything about them.

"Oh, sorry about that," he said. "I dyed my hair last week and didn't notice I'd splashed until the stains had already dried." Then he added, "But it's okay. I wash the stains every morning after my shower because the instructions on the box said it would clean up after 12 to 24 washings."

—BARRY WILSON

I am a lousy bow hunter, a fact that was driven home to me by my ten-year-old niece. Handing me an arrow that she found in the woods, Gina explained, "I figured it was yours. There's no deer on the end of it."

—MARK RUSZALA

Wondering why my niece, Charlotte was returning to college to get a master's in philosophy, I asked, "What can you do with a degree like that?"

"Well," she explained, "it will qualify me to deal with questions like, 'What is existence?' 'What is the essence of things?' and 'Do you want fries with that?'"

—MEL LOFTUS

I had to laugh when I first heard the greeting on my son's answering machine at West Virginia University: "Hi, this is Rick. If you are someone from the phone company, I've already sent the money. If this is one of my parents, please send money. If it's my financial institution, you didn't lend me enough money. If you're a friend, you owe me money. If you are a female . . . I have plenty of money!"

—KRISTIN CLAYTON

"Is this in HD?"

During dinner, I asked my three-year-old granddaughter if her meal was good. She picked over the plate before answering, "Not yet."

—WILLIAM YANNEY

A young French student is sent by his parents to spend a month with an English aristocratic family. His host, the lord of the house, shows him around the estate.

"Is that a golf course over there?" asks the boy. "Do you play often?"

"No," came the reply. "I tried once, but I didn't like it. Too tiring."

The student then sees two horses in a paddock. "I see you ride horses," he says.

"No," the lord replied, "I tried once, but I didn't like it. Too tiring."

The visit continues and they walk past a tennis court. "I suppose that . . ."

"Goodness, no," the lord answered, "I tried once, but I didn't like it. Too tiring."

At that point, a young man walks toward them. "Let me introduce my son, William, to you," says the lord.

The French boy shakes his hand and, turning toward the lord, quips, "An only child, I take it?"

—ROGER KISSEL

A teacher friend of my wife was discussing compound nouns with her class. "They're made up of two or more words," she explained. "For example, town house or boxcar. Can anyone think of another one?"

One boy raised his hand and offered, "Asphalt."

—JOSEPH R. VER BERG

Suffering a migraine attack one night, my sister, Debbie, lay down for a while, leaving her four children to do their homework. However, a short time later a fellow member of her church knocked on the door, and Debbie was horrified to hear one of her kids tell the visitor, "You can't come in. Mom's in bed with a migrant."

—SUE DALITZ

After being a widower for a few years, I was going to remarry. My daughter, with three young sons who had fond memories of their grandmother, tried to explain to them why I was getting married again. "Grandpa's lonely," she said. "He needs someone to talk to, go for walks with. He needs a companion at mealtime and company at home."

Doug, the middle boy, said, "Why doesn't he get a dog?"

—H. B. CLARKE

A few days before Mother's Day, my husband announced he had to work that Sunday and wouldn't be able to fix me dinner as he usually does. "I have an idea," my teenage daughter piped up. "I'll take you out to eat."

"But the restaurants will be so crowded with all the other mothers," I protested.

"Don't worry, Mom," she replied. "Most of them probably won't be eating at McDonald's."

—NANCY DEARBORN

When do cows go to sleep?
When it's pasture bedtime.

HOSS ALLRED

Days after our youngest daughter was born, my family went for a drive. While my wife ran into a store, the baby started to cry. Not having anything else to give her, I let her suck on my finger while we waited for her mother to come back and breast-feed her. My eldest, age four, said, "Is that how you feed her—from your finger?"

—ADAM CAMPBELL

When I met five-year-old Timmy, he was in the hospital with broken legs. He'd chased a ball into the street and was hit by a car. Six weeks later, as his discharge nurse, I asked, "The next time your ball rolls into the street, what will you do?"

Timmy replied, "Send my sister."

—LINDA E. WILLIAMS

Blood may be thicker than water, but baseball beats them both. I learned this after explaining to my two boys that they were half-Lithuanian on their father's side and half-Yankee, meaning their other set of parents came from an old New England family.

My younger son looked worried. "But we're still a hundred percent Red Sox, right, Mom?"

—GAYLA BIEKSHA

"What does the word contemplate mean?" the college student asked his English professor.

"Think about it," the professor answered.

"Ugh!" the student groaned. "Can't you just tell me?"

—DANA THAYER

At a baby shower, everyone was asked to complete nursery rhymes. My 11-year-old daughter, Taylor, contributed this: "Jack Sprat could eat no fat. His wife could eat no carbs."

—DAVID HAM

A nursery-school teacher was driving a station wagon full of kids home one day when a fire truck zoomed past. Sitting in the front seat of the truck was a Dalmatian. The children started discussing the dog's duties.

"They use him to keep crowds back," said one child.

"No," said another. "He's just for good luck."

"No," said a third child. "They use the dogs to find the fire hydrants."

—RAYMONDE BOURGEOIS

When I was a teenager, my father caught me reading one of my older sister's magazines. "Son, why are you reading that sissy magazine?" he asked.

"There's an article that tells women where to meet men," I responded, pointing to the magazine's cover. "I need to know where I'm supposed to be."

—STEVEN C. VAUGHN

When I signed up our four-year-old for floor hockey at the YMCA, I reviewed the rules with him. Steven was used to playing with his older siblings, and I wanted to be sure he wouldn't be too rough when playing with other four-year-olds.

"Under no circumstances," I lectured, "are you allowed to hit anyone with your stick, no matter how mad they make you."

"Don't worry, Mommy," Steven replied. "I know that you drop your stick first and then fight!"

—SHELLEY M. SMITH

"**H**e's going to beat me up!" yelled my four-year-old.

"Why would your older brother do that?" I asked him.

"Because I accidentally dropped his toothbrush in the toilet."

"Just tell him and give him a new one."

"I can't."

"Why?"

"He's in the bathroom brushing his teeth!"

—KATRINA STANFORD

As I was treating my daughter and her family to the buffet at a casino, all the bells and whistles for a winning slot machine began to go off. My seven-year-old grandson was awed. "Wow!" yelled Casey. "This is like Chuck E. Cheese for old people."

—PATRICIA KEYES

When my ten-year-old came home, I could tell something wasn't right.

"What's wrong?" I asked.

He sighed, "There's this kid who's trying to bully me."

"Trying?"

"Well, he's not very good at it."

—VALERIE BEVERLY

My five-year-old daughter, Rylee, was yelling at her younger brother for hitting her. "Troy, did you hit your sister?" I asked.

"No."

"Troy, Santa Claus can tell if you're lying."

He thought about the ramifications of this before asking, **"Can you?"**

—BRIAN SMITH

"Dave? I have big news.
I hope you're in the Lotus position."

MODERN LIFE

When I went inside the station to pay for my tank of gas, I noticed a sign asking patrons to tell the cashier the number of their pump. Even though I was the only customer, I decided to be silly and tell him anyway.

"I'm Number One," I announced.

He smiled. "Well, now. Looks like those motivational tapes are really working for you."

—VIRGINIA WORZALLA

Mom was getting swamped with calls from strangers. The reason? A medical billing service had launched an 800 number that was identical to hers. When she called to complain, they told her to get a new number.

"I've had mine for twenty years," she pleaded. "Couldn't you change yours?"

They refused. So Mom said, "Fine. From now on I'm going to tell everyone who calls that their bill is paid in full." The company got a new number the next day.

—KIM DRAKE

Working on Capitol Hill, my husband was under constant pressure. After one late-night session, he came home exhausted and went straight to bed. When I turned out the light, he sat up in a panic.

"Is everything okay in the house?" he asked.

"Yes, honey," I answered. "I locked the doors and turned down the heat."

"That's good," he said, lying back down, his eyelids heavy. "What about the Senate?"

—MARILYN DAINES

The DVD player had conked out, and we weren't able to watch the movie we'd rented. Then my husband had a brilliant idea: "Why don't we use the PlayStation?"

We pushed all the buttons but couldn't get it to work, so we gave up and went upstairs.

We were reading in bed when our 17-year-old son appeared in our doorway. "Someone left a DVD in my PlayStation," he said.

"We were trying to watch a movie on it," my husband admitted, "but we couldn't get past the parental control screen."

"What a shame," our son said as he smiled and closed the door.

—CONNIE AMES

His residency complete, my friend's son, Dennis, thought about setting up practice in Great Falls, Montana. He liked the town but suggested his wife visit as well. Barely there a day, she came home and announced, "Let's move."

Surprised at her snap judgment, he asked, "Did you look at some homes or even go downtown?"

"Nope."

"What makes you so certain?" Dennis prodded.

"I pulled over to the side of the road outside of town and popped my hood," she explained. "Within a half-hour, a dozen people stopped to help."

—ROBERT KRAJEWSKI

My friend has a bad habit of overdrawing her bank account. One day before we went shopping, I complained about my lack of funds and lamented, "Guess I'll use plastic." Unconcerned, she whipped out her checkbook: **"I'm using rubber."**

—AMANDA HOWARD

A customer called our video-game service line looking for information regarding his console. So I directed him to our website.

"It's www.pan," I said. "That's p as in potato, a as in ant, n as in—"

"Wait!" he interrupted. "I haven't finished typing p as in potato yet."

—GAEL BUCKLEY

Our friend was describing a couple he befriended at the Pentagon. "They're good people," he insisted. Then, by way of illustration:

"They both have security clearance."

—VALERIE MUNNS GATHRIGHT

Maybe snow or sleet won't delay the mail, but there are other factors—like lack of faith in the system. The man ahead of me at the post office was getting forms for temporarily stopping mail delivery and change of address.

"When you've filled them out," suggested the clerk, " bring them here in person so they don't get lost in the mail."

—P. M. CLEPPER

A friend of mine got lost on the way to the Flat Rock Playhouse, a theater in a small North Carolina town. He stopped at a farmhouse where a woman gave him excellent directions. A week later he went back to see another play, got lost again and stopped at the same house. When the woman came to the door, she exclaimed, "You haven't found it yet?"

—TYSON BETTY

Of course I can keep secrets. It's the people I tell them to who can't keep them.

—ANTHONY HADEN-GUEST

We got lucky when we heard the old Piedmont Hotel in Atlanta was getting a facelift and its beautiful maple doors became available for sale as salvage items. We bought several and had them installed in our 19th-century home. Showing a friend around our house, I pointed out, "You know, many of these doors are from the Piedmont Hotel."

He raised an eyebrow. "Most people just take towels."

—BARBARA WOODALL

A big, burly man paid a visit to a pastor's home. "Sir," he said, "I wish to draw your attention to the terrible plight of a poor family. The father is unemployed, and the mother can't work because of the nine children she must raise. They are hungry and soon will be forced onto the street unless someone pays their $500 rent."

"How terrible!" exclaimed the preacher. Touched by the concern of a man with such a gruff appearance, he asked, "May I ask who you are?"

The visitor sobbed, "I'm their landlord."

While I waited outside for my wife to finish her shopping, my energetic toddler was zooming back and forth on the sidewalk, abruptly turning, then stopping.

An older man who'd just dodged her said, "She's a cutie. How old?"

"Two," I replied.

"Just think!" he offered. "In 14 years, she'll drive that way."

—AARON SANDLIN

"It's not that impressive now, but wait until Photoshop!"

While shopping in a supermarket in Florida, I heard over the PA system: "A wallet was found containing a large sum of cash but no identification. Will those laying claim to it please form a double line at the customer service counter."

—HARRY IANNARELLI

One afternoon I was in our living room reading the sports pages. "This pitcher earns $2.2 million a year just for throwing a ball straight," I ranted to my wife. "Anyone can do that." I picked up a rubber ball that was lying next to my chair and threw it at a couch cushion. "Look at that," I bragged. "Bullseye!"

My wife tossed the ball back, and I threw again, hitting dead center. "Two in a row," I cheered. My third toss went wild and ricocheted into one of my wife's favorite pictures, knocking it off the end table. She didn't even look up.

"And that," she said, "is why you make $22,000 a year."

—JIM CHANDLER

While sightseeing in Kentucky, we stopped to take a tour of Mammoth Cave. A visitor in our group, looking up at the huge domed ceiling, asked the guide, "Has there ever been a cave-in?"

"Never," he reassured us. "But if it did, look on the bright side. Where else could you get buried for $2.50?"

—DOUGLAS MAXSON

After a heart-transplant operation, a man was instructed by his doctor to go on a strict diet, give up smoking and get plenty of sleep.

The patient asked, "What about sex?"

"Only with your wife," the doctor replied. "We don't want you getting too excited."

—DERICK KELAART

In our busy household, meals had often consisted of frozen ready meals. Determined to give us a healthier diet, I decided to make a lamb casserole using fresh meat from the butcher, fresh vegetables from the greengrocer and herbs from the garden. After hours in the kitchen, I served it up to an expectant family.

Everyone agreed the food was delicious. "It tastes so good, Mum," declared my son, "that if you hadn't told me you made it yourself, I'd have thought it was one of the frozen ready meals."

—LUCY GRACE

My grandfather raided his savings account to buy himself an advanced satellite TV system. After the installation, he had two huge satellite dishes in his backyard and a monstrous remote control in his hand.

Our entire family was there for the unveiling. Grandpa sat down in his easy chair and started flipping through hundreds of channels from all over the world. We went outside and saw the dishes rotating until they finally came to rest. When we went back into the living room to see what he had decided to watch, we found that he had gone to sleep in his chair.

—MICHAEL C. STONE

Recently launched into the "real world" and shocked by the expenses that came with it, my brother Dustin was complaining about the high cost of auto insurance.

"If you got married," teased my dad, "the premium would be lower."

Dustin smiled. **"That would be like buying an airline just to get free peanuts."**

—AMY DOBBERSTEIN

"The system is down. Anybody remember how to do *anything?*"

At the start of a week-long training class, a colleague was disappointed when he saw how small his hotel room was. He returned to the front desk. "I have a problem with my room," said my friend. "Do you possibly have a smaller one?"

A puzzled clerk asked for his room number, then checked her computer. "I'm sorry, sir, but we don't have a smaller room."

"I knew it!" he said. "I have the smallest room in this hotel!"

The clerk smiled and offered, "Let me see what I can do." My friend spent the week in a suite.

—DAWN RENWICK

A Texan, a Californian and a Seattle native were in a bar when suddenly the Texan grabbed a full bottle of tequila, tossed it into the air and shot it with a pistol. The other patrons shouted their disapproval, wondering why the Texan would waste good tequila. "It's just tequila," he said. "Where I come from, we have lots of it."

Not to be outdone, the Californian tossed a bottle of fine wine into the air and shot it. Again the patrons gasped at such wastefulness. "Where I come from," he told them, "we have plenty of wine."

Next, the Seattle native took out a bottle of beer and guzzled it. Then he threw the bottle into the air, shot the Californian and caught the falling bottle. "Why did you do that?" the hysterical people screamed.

"Where I come from, we have lots of Californians," the Seattle man explained. "But I really feel I should recycle this bottle."

—CHRISTINE LANTIN

During a congressional race in our district, a party loyalist took one of the candidates to a meeting of farm leaders. There he read off a laundry list of the man's qualifications: native Iowan, graduate of an Ivy League college, successful businessman, State Department staffer, and so on. When he finished, a farmer stood up.

"Seems to me it would be a mistake to send this man to Washington," he said. "We ought to keep him around for breeding purposes."

—A. J. PINDER

Every time I almost think humanity will be OK, I see someone struggle with the self-checkout for 20 minutes.

—CAPRICE CRANE, ON TWITTER

Needing to escape her hectic office, my friend fled to the mall, bought a candy bar and then relaxed on a bench next to a businessman. Soon, she heard the sound of a crumpling wrapper and realized that he was eating her candy bar. When he went to work on an ice-cream cone, she leaned over and took a huge lick.

"There!" she declared. She then stormed off to her car, reached into her purse for her keys and pulled out the candy bar she thought he'd eaten.

—ASHLEY OLIPHANT

Airport security confiscated my Bengay.
They accused me of packing heat.

—DAVE WEINBAUM

When my dad, a good ol' boy from the South, visited me in Manhattan, I treated him to dinner at an elegant French restaurant. Since he was out of his element, I ordered for him, choosing the beef bourguignon with a side of polenta, which he loved. That night, I overheard him on the phone with my stepmother. "Dinner was great," he raved. "But you won't believe how much they charge here for pot roast and grits."

—JULIE WEHMEYER

Believe it or not, I just received a check from Medicare for all of one cent. Why, I don't know, but concerned that some arcane regulation—complete with penalty—would apply for not cashing a government check, I took it to the bank. The teller looked at the amount, checked the endorsement and then asked, "How would you like this, heads or tails?"

—SHELDON LEVITAS

This guy is admitted to the hospital. Too weak to speak, he and his roommate sleep for days.

After two weeks, the first man gets the strength to point to himself and say, "American."

His roommate says, "Canadian." Exhausted, they pass out.

Two weeks later, the American summons the strength to speak again. "Shawn," he says in a frail voice.

"Dave," his roommate squeaks. They both fall back into a deep sleep.

Two weeks later, Shawn rouses himself enough to speak. "Cancer," he says.

Dave clears his throat and says, "Sagittarius."

—SHILPA SALGAONKAR

Stuck in traffic and bored out of my wits, I wiled away the time by staring at the back of the truck ahead of me. It belonged to a septic-tank company with a rather distinctive website: www.poophappens.com.

—LUKE SMITH

Nine months pregnant with twins, I bellied up to the supermarket meat bin in search of the perfect roast. The butcher appeared from the back and asked, "May I help you?"

"No, thank you," I said. "I'm just looking."

A minute later, he returned. "Can I help you?"

"No, I'm just looking," I repeated.

A few minutes later, he appeared yet again, asking the same annoying question.

"I'm just looking!" I said testily.

"In that case, ma'am," he said politely, "would you please step back a bit? Your stomach is pressing our service bell."

—SHIRLEY KRASELSKY

I was explaining to my daughter the changes in my political views over the years. When I was in college, I told her, I owned nothing and liked the idea of sharing the wealth, so I was a socialist. After I got married and bought a car, I became a Democrat. Then I got a good job and bought a house, so I became a Republican. As I got older, I invested my savings and made a fair amount of money and became a conservative. And now that I help my family and give money to church and charities, I concluded, I'm not sure what to call myself.

My daughter rolled her eyes and said, "How about *Your Majesty!*"

—BRUCE LAMKEN

AT WORK

"It is impossible to live without failing at something, unless you live so cautiously that you might as well not have lived at all."

—J. K. ROWLING

ON THE JOB

My 21-year-old granddaughter was being interviewed for a job. "What would you describe as your weakness?" she was asked. "Um . . . shoes?"
She got the job.

—MURALI NARAYANAN

A job seeker at my office was filling out an application. After writing in his address, he was asked "Length of residence?"
The applicant wrote "One acre."

—JENNIFER MCNEIL

"Despite your university's outstanding qualifications and previous experience rejecting applicants, I find that your rejection does not meet my needs at this time. Therefore, I will assume the position of assistant professor in your department this August. Good luck rejecting future applicants."

After two stress-filled years of preparing for, then taking, a professional certification test, I got the results in the mail: I passed! Thrilled, I texted my family. My excitement waned somewhat after receiving this reply from my sister: "We are so excited about the news of your passing. Please let us know when the family will be celebrating!"

—REBECCA ATNIP

After I sent out résumés to universities regarding faculty positions, my husband asked if I'd caught the typo, the one where I addressed the cover letter: "Dear Faulty Search Committee."

—JENNIFER GOLBECK

"More applicants from Monster.com!"

The ad on Craigslist for this position explains why it opened up in the first place: **"We need a smart or more person to help un with our Company."**

My wife has been working as a temp in an office since the previous assistant retired. When she went to file some invoices, she was confused to find the M section of the filing cabinet almost full, while the other sections were practically empty. After checking, she realized that the last person had filed all the invoices under "Mr." or "Mrs."

—RAY HEYWOOD

Medical transcription requires a keen ear for technical jargon. But one applicant insisted she was singularly qualified for the position. After all, she wrote in her cover letter, "both of my sisters are nurses, and I watch the cable shows *Dr. G: Medical Examiner* and *Trauma: Life in the E.R.*"

—DONNA FORREST

The boss to one of his staff: "We've got a vacancy. Your twin brother could fill it."

"My twin brother?"

"Yes. The one I saw at the football game yesterday while you were attending your uncle's funeral."

When my sister applied for a job as a flight attendant, she was asked a battery of personal questions, including "Have you ever had a moving violation?"

"Yes," she answered. **"I was evicted two years ago."**

—MARGARET SYMINGTON

The client had a reputation for not paying his bills, but my brother-in-law George took the handyman's job anyway. And when he finished, sure enough, he left with a promise that the check would be in the mail soon. Days later, no check, but he did get called back by the client, who complained of an awful smell coming from the den.

"I have an idea what it might be," said George. "But before I do anything, I need to be paid for the first job."

Desperate, the man paid him on the spot. With that, George walked over to the fireplace and pulled out the dead fish he'd stashed there days earlier.

—WILLIAM LUDEWIG

I ran a store in a small town and often took calls from remote properties asking me to deliver food and other goods to them. On one occasion, I was asked to send a toothbrush.

"Do you want an expensive or a cheap one?" I asked.

"Make it a good one," was the reply. "There are five of us out here."

—JACK GENTLE

My neighbor Ernie pulled into his driveway after a tough day of repairing roofs. He got out of the truck and slammed the door. As his assistant jumped down from the passenger seat, Ernie let him have it.

"Dammit, Dave," he yelled. "I've taught you everything I know, and you still don't know anything!"

—CHRIS ERICKSON

The marquee at our neighborhood Mexican restaurant reads: "Open 24 hours in queso emergency."

—MARY MORA

"Our e-mail is down."

A sign prominently displayed at my workplace:
"Is today the day you become complacent?"

—W.P.

When my husband was a home builder, his thumb ended up on the business end of a sledgehammer, and our three-year-old daughter, Kiana, was eager to tell the entire world. When her caregiver asked how the accident had happened, Kiana shook her head sadly and said, "You know, sometimes at work, my daddy just gets hammered."

—STASIA UHLMANN

Soon after my accident, I went back to the classroom wearing a plaster cast round my chest that couldn't be seen under my shirt.

One day, I was having trouble reining in my rowdy tenth-grade class. Making matters worse, a stiff breeze coming from an open window kept blowing my tie into my face. That, at least, I could control: I stapled the tie onto my plaster cast.

It worked. The pupils' mouths fell open. For the rest of the day, I had no trouble from any of them.

—PAUL MADDOCKS

My first job was at a fine-dining establishment. On the night we ran out of french fries, my boss handed me $100 and told me to run to the McDonald's next door and get $100 worth of fries. But when I came back with two huge greasy sacks, my boss looked confused.

"What's this?" she asked.

"The $100 worth of fries you asked for," I said.

Her eyes narrowed. "I told you $100 in fives!"

—KELLY SEMB

I visited my accountant to pick up an estate-planning form. His assistant was at lunch, so he hunted through the filing cabinet without success. When she returned, he asked for the form. She went straight to the filing cabinet and handed one over.

"How did you file them?" he asked.

"Under S for estate," she said.

—ALEX MCERVALE

Overheard in the HR office: "I need my birth date to log on to my online benefits information.

But I can't remember what year I pretended I was born when you hired me."

—NICOLE HOLT

When I worked at a video store, I mentioned to a customer that her son already had a film out.

"What film?" she asked.

Realizing that it came from the adult section, and too embarrassed to tell her the title, I mumbled, "Uh . . . I'm not sure."

"That's all right," she said, putting her movie back. "I'll just watch whatever he got."

—PAUL BREON

Wanting to look my best for the office party, I splurged on a new dress, strappy high-heel shoes and, to add a fashion statement to my newly pedicured toenails, a toe ring.

That evening, I sashayed into the club, head high, and approached my boss's wife. Pointing to my painted, bejeweled toes, I asked, "Notice anything?"

"Yes," she gushed. "That's quite a bunion you have."

—ZOE SCHREIBMAN

At the end of my missionary work, where I served as the village doctor, the people bid me a warm and tearful farewell.

"Please don't go," an elderly villager pleaded.

Touched, I tried to reassure him. "Don't worry. You will soon get a much better doctor than me here."

"That's what the previous doctor told us."

—DR. A. LAXMINARAYANA RAO

Our supervisor, a saintly grandmother, was toiling away in her cubicle when the human relations specialist dropped by and asked her, in a voice loud enough for all to hear, "Do you have time to discuss your STD?" The room went uncomfortably silent, before she explained, "You know, your Short Term Disability."

—BERND SCHOLZ

After her election, the first Jewish woman president called her mother to invite her to the inauguration. The mother agreed to come, and when the great day arrived she was seated among Supreme Court justices and cabinet members.

Just a short time into the solemn ceremony, she nudged the man to her left. "You see that girl with her hand on the Bible?" the mother said with great excitement. "Her brother's a doctor!"

—PETER S. LANGSTON

While making my postal rounds, I delivered bulk mail from an insurance company addressed to "The safe driver at . . ."

The next day, one of my customers kicked the envelope back to me after having written on it, **"No such person at this address."**

—JOHN REDDY

Adding a funny hat to your pajamas at home—weird.
Adding a funny hat to your pajamas at work—chef.

—COMEDIAN JULIEANNE SMOLINSKI

The mayor of a city in a developing country invited the mayor of another municipality over for dinner. The visitor was very impressed with his host's affluent lifestyle and asked him how he managed to live so well. "See that bridge?" the first mayor said, pointing to a distant structure. "I skimmed five percent."

The visiting mayor went home and six months later invited the first mayor over to his new mansion. The first mayor was astounded and asked his friend the secret to his sudden wealth.

"See that bridge?" the second mayor said, gesturing out the window.

"What bridge?" asked the visitor.

"One hundred percent."

—ATUL T. SURAIYA

My father, who edited engineering proposals, got into a heated argument with an inflexible engineer. At the root of it was the latter's description of a harbor waterway project. He'd written: ". . . and there shall be three berths, each with its own berth control tower."

—DAVID USHER

These businesses know it's all in how they sell themselves:

- Ad from a local gym: "If you're not satisfied with the results at our club, we'll give you your old body back."

  —ELEANOR GUYNN

- Sign spotted at a shoe store: "If we don't have your size, it's free!"

  —STUART MCLENNAN

●　●　●　●　●　●　●　●　●　●　●　●　●　●　●　●

I think my fellow EMTs rely too heavily on abbreviation when they write their reports. One read: "Medic broke wind, and entered residence."

—D.B.

In the newsletters for the town house complex I manage, I always reiterate the rules, especially the one about cleaning up litter and debris. Unfortunately, my choice of words is not always the best. I once wrote "It is the resident's responsibility to keep their private area clean. Please refer to the rules and regulations if you don't know where your private area is."

—KELLY FRAMPTON

"How are things going?" one bee asked another.

"Terrible," the second bee replied. "I can't find any flowers or pollen anywhere."

"No problem," said the first bee. "Just fly down this street until you see all the cars. There's an outdoor bar mitzvah going on with lots of flower arrangements and fresh fruit."

"Thanks!" said the second bee, buzzing off.

Later, the two bees ran into one another, and the second bee thanked the first bee for the tip.

The first bee asked, "But what's that thing on your head?"

"My yarmulke," the second bee replied. "I didn't want them to think I was a wasp."

—LAURA BARILOTTI

What's gray, crispy and hangs from the ceiling?

An amateur electrician.

———————————————————————— DOC BLAKELY

Personally, I don't believe the world owes me a living—although for the amount I get, an apology would be nice.

Carpenters from California, Missouri and New York showed up at the White House for a tour. The chief guard welcomed them with special enthusiasm because the front gates were in need of repair. He asked each person to come up with a bid. The California carpenter measured and figured and finally said, "Well, $400 for materials, $400 for my crew and $100 profit for me, $900 total." The guard nodded and turned to the carpenter from Missouri.

That man took out his tape measure and a pencil and after some calculating said, "It'll cost $700—$300 each for materials and my crew and $100 profit for me." The guard thanked the man and turned to the carpenter from New York.

Without hesitation, the New Yorker said, "This job will run $2700."

The guard gasped. "You didn't even measure or do any calculating," he replied. "How do you figure it'll be so expensive?"

"Simple," said the New York carpenter. "$1000 for me, $1000 for you, and we hire the guy from Missouri."

—DAN ANDERSON

Real estate agents are pulling out all the stops to sell homes. One particularly ingenious marketing ploy promised: "Free coffee with any purchase."

—MATTHEW KORNEGAY

A fellow teacher left the restroom and said, "You know you work in an elementary school when the graffiti on the bathroom wall says, 'I love my mom.'"

—LYNNETTE LOTT

"How's this for a severance package—five minutes to grab all you can get."

Four friends were arguing over whose dog was the smartest.

The first man, an engineer, called to his dog, "T Square, show your stuff." The dog trotted over to a desk, pulled out a paper and pencil and drew a perfect triangle.

The next guy, an accountant, called to his dog, "Slide Rule, go ahead." The canine went to the kitchen, nibbled open a bag of cookies and divided the contents into four equal piles.

The next man, a chemist, beckoned his dog, Beaker, to show what he could do. The dog went to the fridge, took out a quart of milk and poured out exactly eight ounces into a measuring cup.

The last man was a government worker. "Coffee Break," he hollered to his dog, "go to it." With that, the dog jumped to his feet, soiled the paper, ate the cookies and drank the milk.

—PAMELA JASON

While I was performing in a show outside Chicago, there was a gentleman who could often be found hanging around the lobby. Everyone called him the Marquis. One day, I asked the artistic director if he'd gotten the nickname because he looked so distinguished. "No," he replied. "We call him the Marquee because he hangs out in front of the theater and is usually lit."

—MARK REANEY

Overheard:

Sam: I used to be a stand-up comedian before I worked here.
Joe: I never would have guessed that.
Sam: Ask me why I quit.
Joe: Why did you . . .
Sam: Timing!
Joe: . . . quit?

—MIKE SMITH

The insurance industry loves its acronyms. The first time I saw the term proof of ownership was in a client's file that read: "Insured has POO on damaged items."

—AMANDA SCHAEFER

How bad is business in our area?
A sign on an office building declared,

"Buy one building, get one free."

—JAN PEARSON

The secretary to her boss on the intercom: "There's a gentleman on the line who would like to inquire into the secret of your success."

After a prolonged silence, the boss asks in a hoarse voice: "Is he a journalist or a policeman?"

—ALDA FERREIRA ANTUNES

One coworker's advice to another: "It's one thing to stick your neck out for a person, but when you stick your neck out for a system, it's just a waste of neck."

—KATHRYN HARGROVE

Two friends were discussing their family histories when one of them lamented that he knew precious little about his roots. "I've always wanted to have my family history traced," he said, "but I can't afford to hire someone. Any suggestions?"

"Sure," replied his friend. **"Run for public office."**

—EARLE HITCHNER

Why teachers take the summer off . . .

Teacher: What does the word plummet mean?
Eight-year-old student: A girl plumber.

—JACLYN TISCHHAUSER

Our cable customer complained that his service was acting up. When I asked what the trouble was, he explained, "Connectile dysfunction."

—ROBERT MCCULLOUGH

While my brother, a helicopter pilot, was attending a training exercise, another chopper pilot prematurely released his payload and dropped it 300 feet to the ground. No one was hurt, but the next morning, this label was placed next to the release switch on all the copters: For Desk Job, Push Here.

—VIRGINIA SPENCER

"Do you believe in life after death?" the boss asked one of his employees.

"Yes," replied the employee.

"That's okay then," said the boss. "Because while you were at your grandmother's funeral yesterday, she popped in to see you."

—GERALD MCDADE

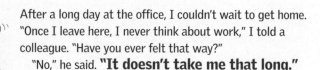

After a long day at the office, I couldn't wait to get home. "Once I leave here, I never think about work," I told a colleague. "Have you ever felt that way?"

"No," he said. **"It doesn't take me that long."**

—STEVE BENNETT

QUOTABLE QUOTES

"WHEN A MAN TELLS YOU THAT HE GOT RICH THROUGH HARD WORK, ASK HIM: 'WHOSE?'"

—DON MARQUIS

"You go to your TV to turn your brain off. You go to the computer when you want to turn your brain on."

—STEVE JOBS

"Confidence is 10 percent hard work and 90 percent delusion."

—TINA FEY, IN *VOGUE*

"A professional is one who does his best work when he feels the least like working."

—FRANK LLOYD WRIGHT

"I read about a new 24-hour daycare that's opening in India. Yeah, it's pretty cute: Instead of playing telephone, the kids just play tech support."

—JIMMY FALLON, ON *LATE NIGHT*

"I couldn't wait for success, so I went ahead without it."

—JONATHAN WINTERS

"I USED TO WANT TO BE A LAWYER, BUT I DIDN'T WANT TO HAVE HALF MY BRAIN SUCKED OUT."

—MAX WALKER

"Be nice to nerds. Chances are you'll end up working for one."

—CHARLES SYKES

"Hard work never killed anybody, but why take a chance?"

—EDGAR BERGEN

"IN THE BUSINESS WORLD, THE REARVIEW MIRROR IS ALWAYS CLEARER THAN THE WINDSHIELD."

—WARREN BUFFET

" 'PUL OVR.' You mean that was from you? "

LAW AND DISORDER

A cop stops a drunk late at night and asks where he's going.

"I'm going to a lecture about alcohol abuse and the effects it has on the human body," slurs the drunk.

"Really? Who's giving that lecture at one in the morning?"

"My wife."

—ALFRED MANSOOR

Recently, my husband was pulled over for not wearing his seat belt. But Irv was convinced he was being railroaded.

"Officer," he said in his most condescending voice. "How do you know I'm not wearing a seat belt if my windows are tinted?"

"Because, sir," replied the officer, "it's hanging out the door."

—JUDITH FINKLER

A man went to the police station and asked to speak to the burglar who had broken into his house the previous night.

"You'll get your chance in court," the desk sergeant told him.

"I have to know how he got into the house without waking my wife," pleaded the man. "I've been trying to do that for years!"

—SUZANNE DEVONSHIRE

The police stops a car on the freeway and asks the driver: "Sir, may I ask for how long have you been driving with defective back lights?"

The driver gets out, looks at the back of his car, then falls on his knees and begins to sob.

"Oh come on," the policeman consoles him, "it's not so serious as that."

"Oh no? And my trailer and motorboat? Where are they?"

—ERIKA ANTALNÉ FILUS

A police officer at the scene of a car accident saw a horrible sight smashed against the inside of the windshield. Quickly he called for help and then ran over to the car.

"Are you badly hurt?" the officer asked the man in the front seat.

"Nah," replied the driver, "but this pizza is a mess."

—TIM CARVER

The irate driver waved his speeding ticket in the air at the police officer who'd just written him up.

"What am I supposed to do with this?" the man yelled.

"Hang on to it," the cop replied.

"When you collect four, you get a bicycle."

—MARILYN MACDONALD

The police stop a motorist for a roadside check.

"What are all those daggers in your car?" the trooper asks.

"I'm a juggler."

"I don't believe it," the policeman says, "show me something."

The juggler gets out and starts tossing the daggers.

Another car passes by with two buddies in it. Says one: "Boy, I'm glad I quit drinking. Look what they've come up with in place of a breathalyzer."

—MARGIT MOLNÁR

When a neighbor's home was burglarized, I decided to be more safety conscious. But my measly front-door lock wasn't going to stop anyone, so I hung this sign outside: "Nancy, don't come in. The snake is loose. Mom."

—SHARON BOUSCHER

▾ ▾ ▾ ▾ ▾ ▾ ▾ ▾ ▾ ▾ ▾ ▾ ▾ ▾ ▾ ▾

A male and female driver are involved in a horrific collision. Amazingly, both escape unhurt, though their cars are written off.

As they crawl from the wreckage, the man sees the woman is blonde and beautiful. She turns to him and gushes breathily: "We shouldn't have survived that. Maybe it's a sign from God that we're meant to be together!"

Sensing he could be on to a good thing, the man stammers back, "Oh yes, I agree completely!"

"And look," she continues. "Though my car was destroyed, this bottle of wine is intact, too! It's another sign. Let's drink to our love!"

"Well, okay!" says the man, going with the moment. She offers him the bottle, so he downs half and hands it back. "Your turn," he says.

"No, thanks," says the woman, "I think I'll just wait for the police."

A man notices that his wife is missing. He goes to the police station to file a report. The officer on duty asks him to describe her.

"Okay," he says, "but only on one condition. You cannot show it to her afterward."

—TÍMEA LÁDI

A report came into the police station about a house break-in and the theft of five bagpipes. The desk sergeant took the information and said, "We'll send out an investigator." Then, turning the complaint over to one of his officers, he suggested, **"I'd check out the neighbors on either side."**

—JACK TRACY

The police arrived and found a woman dead on her living room floor with a golf club next to her body.

An officer asked the husband, "Is this your wife?"

"Yes," he replied.

"Did you kill her?"

"Yes," he replied.

"It looks like you struck her eight times with this 3-iron. Is that correct?"

"Yes," the husband replied, "but put me down for a five."

—GRAHAME JONES

I was prosecuting a case involving a man charged with driving under the influence. The defense counsel was beginning to lose his cool with the police witnesses and implied that they had gotten their facts wrong.

"People do make mistakes, don't they, Officer Lock?" he demanded of one witness.

"Yes, sir," came the reply. "I'm Officer Webster."

The defense lost.

—ROGER GRAY

While fishing off a beach in the Caribbean, a lawyer struck up a conversation with an engineer. The lawyer explained that his house had burnt down and he had lost everything. Happily, though, the insurance company had paid out a sizeable sum for the damage.

"That's a coincidence," remarked the engineer. "My house and all my belongings were destroyed in a flood, and my insurance company also coughed up for everything."

The lawyer looked confused. "How do you start a flood?" he asked.

—ROHAN CHOPRA

**"It's bad enough I get overruled at home—
but here also, Sharon?"**

The prosecutor was relentless as he badgered the witness. "What did the accused do when he learned the jewelry was part of a stolen hoard?" he demanded.

"He did what any honest man would do," said the witness.

"And what was that?"

"I didn't think you'd know."

—GENE NEWMAN

> Walking into a lawyer's office, a man asked what the barrister's rates were.
>
> "Fifty dollars for three questions," the lawyer stated.
>
> "Isn't that awfully expensive?" the man asked.
>
> "Yes," the lawyer replied. **"What's your third question?"**
>
> —MATT FRANKLIN

The murder suspect's trial wasn't going well, so his attorney resorted to a trick. "Ladies and gentlemen of the jury," he said, "I have a surprise for you. In one minute, the real murderer will walk into this courtroom."

Stunned, the jurors looked toward the door, but nothing happened. The lawyer chuckled.

"I lied. But because you all looked with anticipation, that proves there is reasonable doubt as to my client's guilt, and I insist that you find him not guilty."

The jury retired to deliberate, then returned a verdict of guilty.

"But you must have had some doubt," bellowed the lawyer. "You all stared at the door."

"Oh, we looked," said the jury foreman. "But your client didn't."

—SARAH BROWN

I mentioned to an unmarried friend of mine—an attorney—that he should attend a singles mixer for lawyers. He hated the idea.

"Why," he asked, "would I want to date someone who's been trained to argue?"

—AUGUST MURPHY

It had been a nerve-wracking experience for my attorney husband. He was working with the FBI on a federal sting operation. Worried for his safety, they put him under protective surveillance. Finally the agency told him they had rounded up all the criminals and were lifting the surveillance. A few days later my relieved spouse was on the phone, telling his brother about the whole adventure.

"Did you happen to mention to the FBI that you have an identical twin?" his horrified brother interrupted. "Who lives next door?"

—J.D.

At a courtroom, the judge interrogates the defendant, "So, you declare you suffer from a disease that affects your memory?"

"That's right," answers the defendant.

"And how does this disease affect you?"

"It makes me forget things."

"So, could you give us an example of something you've forgotten?"

—CARMEM MARIA F. LIMA

I work in a courthouse, so when I served jury duty, I knew most of the staff. As I sat with other prospective jurors listening to a woman drone on about how long the process was taking, a judge and two lawyers passed by, giving me a big hello. A minute later, a few maintenance workers did the same. That set off the malcontent: "Just how long have you been serving jury duty?"

—KATHLEEN DERBY STURDIVANT

Where do vampires learn to suck blood?
Law school.

MARILYN MILLER

A group of prospective jurors was asked by the judge whether any of them felt they had ever been treated unfairly by an officer of the law.

"I once got a ticket for running a stop sign," offered one woman, "even though I definitely came to a complete stop."

"Did you pay the ticket?" the judge questioned.

"Yes."

"If you thought you were innocent," the judge went on, "why didn't you contest it?"

"Your Honor," she replied, "there have been so many times I didn't get a ticket for running a stop sign that I figured this evened things out a little."

—CHARLES KRAY

JURY OF ONE'S PEARS

●　●　●　●　●　●　●　●　●　●　●　●　●　●　●

**My father still keeps the first dollar he ever made—
and the police still keep the machine he made it with.**

—NATALIA SKORUBSKI

I was in small-claims court when I listened in on the case of a
woman who held a good job but still had trouble paying her bills
on time. "Can't you live within your income?" asked the judge.

"No, Your Honor," she said. "It's all I can do to live within
my credit."

—RALPH WARTH

A woman is brought to court after stealing from a supermarket.

"Mrs. Krupnick," says the judge, "what did you take?"

"Just a small can of peaches," she answers. "There were only
six peaches in the can."

"Six peaches . . . hmm . . . I sentence you to six nights in jail,
a night for each peach."

The woman is crushed. She's about to collapse to the floor
when her husband, seated in the gallery, leaps to his feet.

"Your Honor," he shouts, "she also stole a can of peas!"

Farmer Joe is suing a trucking company over injuries he
suffered in an auto accident.

The company's lawyer begins his cross-examination. "Is it
true that at the accident scene you said, 'I'm fine'?"

"Let me explain," pleads the farmer. "I had loaded my mule
Bessie into the trailer and was driving down the road when this
truck crashed into us. I was hurt bad. When the trooper came
on the scene, he heard Bessie moaning. He took one look at her,
pulled out his gun and shot her right between the eyes.

"Then he walked over to me with his gun and asked, 'Your
mule was in such bad shape I had to shoot her. How are you?' "

I grew up in the Midwest and was very unsure of myself when I went to take the road test for my driver's license. The examiner was a woman who said nothing to me the entire time, except for giving terse instructions to turn left, right and parallel park.

When we returned to the parking lot, she looked at me. "I'm going to give you your license," she said. "But don't ever ask to borrow my car."

—MARILYN CASEY

A priest, a doctor and a lawyer were stuck behind a particularly slow group of golfers. After three holes, they complained to the greenskeeper.

"Sorry, guys. That's a group of blind firefighters," the man explained. "They lost their sight saving our clubhouse from burning down last year, so we let them play here anytime for free."

"That's so sad," the priest said. "I'll say a special prayer for them tonight."

"Good idea," the doctor agreed. "I'm going to contact my ophthalmologist buddy and see if there's anything he can do for them."

"I guess," the lawyer said. "But why can't they play at night?"

"There's good news and bad news," the divorce lawyer told his client.

"I could sure use some good news," sighed the client. "What is it?"

"Your wife isn't demanding that your future inheritances be included in the settlement."

"And the bad news?"

"After the divorce, she's marrying your father."

—STEVE KEUCHEL

"**W**hy do you want to divorce your wife?" demands the judge.

"Because every night she whispers in my ear: 'It's time for you to go home.'"

—FERENC L.

An airliner was having engine trouble, and the pilot instructed the cabin crew to have the passengers take their seats and prepare for an emergency landing. A few minutes later the pilot asked the flight attendants if everyone was buckled in and ready.

"All set back here," came the reply, "except for one lawyer who's still passing out business cards."

— BRYAN STINCHFIELD

One day, First Lady Eleanor Roosevelt visited a penitentiary. When FDR asked where she was, he was told, "She's in prison."

"I'm not surprised," Roosevelt responded. "But what for?"

A letter I received while presiding over traffic court: "Dear Judge, I am sorry to be so slow in sending in the money for my traffic ticket. But having gotten recently married, I am just getting back on my feet."

—JAMES R. WALTON

During his spare time my brother, an attorney, volunteers on his town's fire and rescue squad. When I mentioned this to a friend, he smiled and said, "Let me get this straight. Your brother is a lawyer and an EMT? **So he doesn't have to chase the ambulance—he's already in it?**"

—DALE BIRCH

TECH TALK

The computer in my high school classroom was acting up. After watching me struggle with it, a student explained that my hard drive had crashed. So I called IT. "Can someone look at my computer?" I asked. "The hard drive crashed."

"We can't just send people down on your say-so," said the specialist. "How do you know that's the problem?"

"A student told me."

"We'll send someone right over."

—THOMAS ELLSWORTH

My heart sank as I read the spam that began, "By opening this e-mail, you have activated the Amish computer virus." Then I realized that not only was my computer in jeopardy, so was my reputation, as it continued, "Since the Amish don't have computers, this works on the honor system. Please delete all your files. Thank you."

—TRACIE WALKER

Outraged by the high fees her computer consultants charged, a friend asked my dad which service he used. "My sons," he said. "They both have degrees in computer science."

"So you get that kind of work done for nothing," the friend marveled.

Dad smiled. "Actually, I figured it cost me about $40,000 for my kids to fix my computer for free."

—RYAN GILLESPIE

A computer once beat me at chess, but it was no match for me at kickboxing.

—EMO PHILIPS

I finally convinced my mother that it was a good idea for her to learn to text. Her first message to me: "Whereisthespacebar?"

—CINDY RODEN

Using my cell phone to access the Internet, I was plagued by pop-up ads. Blocking them required a confusing process that ended with this confirmation: "Your cell phone number has been added to be removed."

—CRAIG YOUNG

A fuming customer called the shop from where he'd bought his new laptop. "You've cheated me," he told the salesgirl. "I can't transfer a single file from my old PC to this one."

"Please tell me what you did," said the salesgirl.

"Oh, you think I don't know?" said the customer. "Okay . . . I right-clicked the mouse on the filename in my old PC and selected the Copy option. I then clicked Paste on the new laptop."

"So did you first get the file into a pen-drive or something?" the confused salesgirl enquired.

"No. I disconnected the mouse and plugged it into the lousy laptop you sold me."

—ISHITA JAIN

I took a two-year-old computer in to be repaired, and the guy looked at me as though he was a gun dealer and I'd brought him a musket. In two years, I'd gone from cutting-edge to Amish.

—JON STEWART

Heating water for pasta, I kept checking to see if it had begun to boil. My 13-year-old son shook his head. "Stop doing that, Mom. It's like that saying: 'A watched website never loads.'"

—JANIE HANSON

While lobbying for her very own computer, my 12-year-old niece asked her father, "When you were a kid, how old were you when you got your own computer?"

"There were no computers when I was a kid," he said.

She was aghast. **"Then how did you get on the Internet?"**

—HERBERT BUETOW

What is a computer's first sign of old age?
Loss of memory.

As a debate arose over a question in our literature class, my professor turned to his iPhone. Scrolling through the search results, he wondered aloud, "What did professors do before Wikipedia?"

A fellow student shouted out, "Know things."

—DANIEL MITCHELL

"I'm thinking of buying a tanning bed," I told my mother-in-law.

"You should talk to my son's friend Craig to see if he has one. Apparently, he's selling all his belongings on the Internet."

Confused, I walked away, wondering, Who do we know named Craig? Then it hit me—Craigslist.

—JENNIFER GILBERT

I've invented Twofacebook, the antisocial network. You start being friends w/entire world & defriend people one by one.

—ANDY BOROWITZ, ON TWITTER

My mother is still having trouble understanding just how her iPhone works. Upon receiving a text, she said to me, "Quick, give me a pencil so I can write this down."

—SANDRA NOVELLA

A man tells his doctor, "Doc, help me. I'm addicted to Twitter!"

The doctor replies, "Sorry, I don't follow you . . ."

—CHRISTINE SCHRUM

"Don't look now . . . I think we're being followed!"

One of my third graders came to school sobbing.

"My son's upset because he couldn't complete his math homework," explained his mother, holding his hand.

"Why?" I asked.

"Unfortunately," she said, "Our computer doesn't have Roman numerals."

—MARSHALL LERESCHE

During the Cold War, I was an interpreter in the air force. We were testing a computer that purportedly could translate Russian into English, and vice versa. We began by uttering this English phrase, "The spirit is willing, but the flesh is weak."

The Russian translation came out, "Vodka horosho, no myaca slabie." Or, in English, "The alcohol is good, but the meat is poor."

—SAM CONNOR

FACEBOOK VS. DAD

David D.: Where to buy chicken casserole supplies
Stephen D.: Dad, this is Facebook, not Google. Try again.
David D.: Where to buy chicken casserole supplies
Stephen D.: Dad, no.
David D.: Where to buy supplies for chicken casserole
Stephen D.: Are you serious?
David D.: Chicken casserole supply store
Stephen D.: Fiesta Mart, 8130 Kirby Drive.

Saddam Hussein decided that he wanted to document his memoirs, so he asked his guard for a stenographer.

The guard came back a little while later with a laptop computer instead.

"No thanks," Saddam said. "I'm a dictator."

—GORDON HALSEY

The Department of Defense has a Contact Us link on its website, inviting readers to pose any question they want. One guy did just that: "So do you have any top secret information you would like to tell me? I am doing a project for my senior economics class and was just wondering. . . . E-mail me back."

—CHRIS PIETRAS

I recently found this great website that conducts cyber garage sales. You list the stuff you want in the subject line of an e-mail, send it off and wait for a response. Recently, I sent a note saying I was in the market for three particular items. In short order, I got three responses. Nobody had any of the items I'd listed. But they all found what I'd written amusing: "Wanted—Envelopes, piano bench and one night stand."

—SANDI SIMMONS

Recently, I eavesdropped on two women chatting.

Woman 1: I just joined an online dating website.
Woman 2: Really? Did you find any matches?
Woman 1: Yeah, my ex-husband.

—YOLANDA GOMEZ

After a minor accident, my mother accompanied me to the emergency room. Now, I'm five feet, three inches tall and pleasantly plump—not exactly Brad Pitt. But when the nurse asked for my height and weight, I blurted out, "Five-foot-eight and 125 pounds."

As the nurse paused to check her eyesight, Mom leaned over to me. "Sweetheart," she gently chided, "this isn't the Internet."

—BOB MEYERSON

Not only am I getting better at Tetris, but I'm loading more dishes into my dishwasher than I ever thought possible.

—COMEDIAN PEGGY O'BRIEN

My wife and I had been texting back and forth when unbeknownst to her, I had to stop for a few minutes. When I returned to my cell phone, I found this text message awaiting me: "CGYT?"

"Huh?" I responded.

She shot back: "Cat Got Your Thumb?"

—PAUL BROUN

What do you get when you cross a rabbit with the Internet?

A hare net.

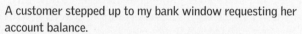

A customer stepped up to my bank window requesting her account balance.

"Sorry," I told her, "but I'm afraid our computer is down."

"Ah," she said understandingly. **"Terminal depression."**

—ADAM PARRY

Some texts should not be abbreviated. Case in point, this message from my cousin, which simply read "A J D." I was confused until my father called to tell me, "Aunt June died."

—MELODIE DIAZ CRUZ

My niece in college posted her latest Facebook status: "I am going home so Mom can take me to the doctor and tell him what's wrong with me."

—VIKKI SMITH

The Last Facebook status update:

- . . . standing over a patient in the operating room, scalpel in hand, wishing he hadn't lied on his résumé about being a surgeon. Here goes nothing . . .

- . . . in a marriage-counseling session with his wife, wondering what the score of the football game is. Go, Eagles!

- . . . thinks that if his boss doesn't like him sleeping on the floor of the office, then his boss shouldn't have gotten such comfy carpets.

- . . . needs help robbing the bank over on the corner of Main and Willow. Any takers? Be there around noonish.

—FRANK FERRI

My ex and I had a very amicable divorce. I know this because when I wrote the Facebook status "I'm getting a divorce," he was the first one to click Like.

—COMEDIAN GIULIA ROZZI

Usually there's no computer problem I can't solve.
But I met my match when I turned on my machine and was greeted with the message

"Keyboard not detected. Hit any key to continue."

—ALEX HU

"Wow!" said my tween daughter. She was reading the nutritional label on a bag of cheese curls. "These must be loaded with cholesterol. The label lists it as Omg!"

My tween son took a look. "That's zero milligrams, not 'Oh My God.'"

—KATHY TORRENCE

Soon after texting a girl I liked, I received this response: "ERROR 3265 SWRVICE UNAVAILABLE." She never could spell.

—CHRISTOPHER THOMPSON

I just read a great novel on my Kindle. It was a real button-presser.

—PETER BACANIN

How do you make friends with a computer?
Bit by bit.

" Let's face it . . . we're dial-up people in a broadband world. "

"What are those?" asked my younger sister. She had just spotted the old encyclopedias our mother had unearthed in the basement.

Mom tried to explain the concept of an encyclopedia to her, but it just wasn't clicking. She finally blurted out, "It's like Google, but in a book."

—AMBER SANDOE

My father just e-mailed me a note: "This e-mail is from my new computer. Does it look better? Love, Dad."

—JANICE KYLE

I didn't realize how good I was with computers until I met my parents.

—COMEDIAN MIKE BIRBIGLIA

What's the biggest problem Facebookers are confronting? Parents signing up. Here's how one writer's Facebook status updates now read, ever since he was friended by his mom:

- Scott is making good, well-informed decisions.

- Scott is going to bed at a very reasonable hour.

- Scott is drinking only on occasion, and even then it's just one or two.

- Scott quit smoking several months ago without any apparent difficulty.

- Scott is making large, regular contributions to his savings account.

- Scott is making yet another home-cooked meal, avoiding fast food as usual.

- Scott is not gaining weight, and his clothes fit just fine.

—SCOTT A. HARRIS

LIFE and DEATH

"All the art of living lies in a fine mingling of letting go and holding on."

—HAVELOCK ELLIS

WHAT'S UP, DOC?

The man goes to see his doctor because he has a lettuce leaf sticking out of his ear.

"Hmmm," the doctor says. "That's strange."

The guy replies, "I know. And that's just the tip of the iceberg."

—GREG COX

Carpooling to work, a man got increasingly stressed with each trip. After a week of panic attacks, he went to the doctor. "I'm fine on the bridges, in the traffic and even in the dark after a long day," the man explained. "But when I go through tunnels with those four other guys, I feel like I'm gonna explode. Am I crazy?"

"Not at all," the doc said. "You just have Carpool Tunnel Syndrome."

—NOAH HART

Two surgeons and a dermatologist were having lunch in the hospital cafeteria when the first two doctors began to laugh hysterically.

"What's so funny?" the dermatologist asked, confused.

"Sorry, you wouldn't understand," one of the surgeons said. "It's an inside joke."

—ANDREW HARGADO

I sat in the doctor's waiting room watching a young mother try desperately to control her three loud children.

"They're not a very good advertisement, are they?" she groaned apologetically.

A man muttered, "Only if you're advertising contraceptives."

—BARBARA WOOTTON

❝You're right. Without fail, it's tied inversely proportionally to the Dow.❞

To treat my bronchitis, the doctor pulled out his prescription pad.

"This is for Zithromax," he said as he wrote, then muttered, "Mypenzadyne."

I was familiar with the antibiotic Zithromax but not the other drug. "What's Mypenzadyne?"

He looked confused for a second, then enunciated slowly, "My pen is dying."

—JASON ARMSTRONG

Did you hear about the student who flunked medical school? **His handwriting was legible.**

—SAMUEL SILVER

Quasimodo goes to a doctor for his annual checkup. "I think something is wrong with your back," the doctor says.

"What makes you say that?" Quasimodo asks.

"I don't know," the doctor replies. "It's just a hunch."

While making rounds, a doctor points out an X-ray to a group of interns. "As you can see," she says, "the patient limps because his left fibula and tibia are radically arched. Michael, what would you do in a case like this?"

"Well," ponders the intern, "I suppose I'd limp too."

—TRAVIS CRAM

Dad arrived promptly at 9:30 for his appointment with the proctologist. An hour and a half later, he finally saw the doctor. Afterward, the doctor gave him this advice: Avoid sitting for a long time. Dad grumbled, "The only time I do that is when I come here for an appointment."

—MARK GOULDING

We brought our newborn son, Adam, to the pediatrician for his first checkup. As he finished, the doctor told us, "You have a cute baby."

Smiling, I said, "I bet you say that to all new parents."

"No," he replied, "just to those whose babies really are good-looking."

"So what do you say to the others?" I asked.

"He looks just like you."

—MATT SLOT

It had been a long time—seven years to be exact—since my friend Brian had been to see his doctor. So the nurse told him that if he wanted to make an appointment, he would have to be reprocessed as a new patient.

"Okay," said Brian, "reprocess me."

"I'm sorry," she told him. "We're not accepting any new patients."

—BARBARA SAMPSON

Five years had passed since my last eye exam, and I could tell it was definitely time for another. My vision was getting fuzzier. The eye doctor's receptionist gave me a pre-examination form. One entry was "Reason for visiting the doctor." I couldn't resist. I wrote, "Long time no see."

—DAWN ARTESE

In hindsight, I should have been more specific. I was visiting my doctor as part of a checkup after surgery. "When can I resume regular activities?" I asked.

He blushed slightly. "You mean like sex?"

"Actually, I was thinking of vacuuming."

—PATTY KEBERLE

Just before I was to have a physical, my doctor handed me an examining gown.

"I can never remember with these things," I commented. "Does the opening go in the front or the back?"

He shrugged. **"Doesn't matter. You can't win either way."**

—KATHRYN FOLSOM

“ He came out of the surgery okay, but Mr. Sims is on his
way back to the recovery room after seeing the *BILL.* **”**

As soon as I stepped into the urgent-care facility in my hometown, I could see the place was packed with patients. The nurses and doctors all seemed frazzled. Just how frazzled I discovered when a doctor walked into the room, pulled out his examination light, pointed it in my ear and instructed, "Say, 'Ah.'"

—KRISTIN EGERTON

The huge backlog in the doctor's waiting room was taking its toll. Patients were glancing at their watches and getting restless.

Finally, one man walked to the receptionist's station and tapped on the glass.

She slid back the window, saying, "Sir, you'll have to wait your turn."

"I just had a question," he said dryly. "Is George W. Bush still president?"

—DICK FLOERSHEIMER

Panicking when her two-year-old swallowed a tiny magnet, my friend Phyllis rushed him to the emergency room.

"He'll be fine," the doctor promised her. "The magnet should pass through his system in a day or two."

"How will I be sure?" she pressed.

"Well," the doctor suggested, "you could stick him on the refrigerator, and when he falls off, you'll know."

—MARIE THIBODEAU

What did the green grape say to the purple grape?
Breathe! Breathe!

PAUL LEWIS

○ ● ○ ● ○ ● ○ ● ○ ● ○ ● ○ ● ●

I was dancing at a party when I tripped and stubbed my toe. A few days later, my toe swollen and purple, I went to see a podiatrist. I told him how I hurt myself and admitted to feeling foolish at how clumsy I was. X-rays showed my toe was not broken, and the doctor said he didn't need to do anything. Anxious to speed the healing, though, I asked whether there was something I could do: "Should I soak it? Put it on ice? Is there anything you recommend?"

He smiled: "Take dancing lessons."

—BARBARA NANESS

The cardiologist at the ER had bad news for me: "You're going to need a pacemaker."

Later, the nurse filling out the admission form began to ask me the standard questions: "Have you ever had mumps, measles, etc.?"

Seeing how upset I was, she put down the clipboard and took my hand. "Don't worry," she said soothingly. "This kind of heart problem is easily fixed, and your life will be much better as a result."

I felt reassured until she continued: "Do you have a living will?"

—ROBERT PORTER

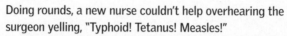

Doing rounds, a new nurse couldn't help overhearing the surgeon yelling, "Typhoid! Tetanus! Measles!"

"Why does he keep doing that?" she asked a colleague.

"Oh, he likes to call the shots around here."

—HEATHER BRESS

After I warned the nurse taking blood that it would be very hard to find a vein on me, she said, "Don't worry. We've seen worse. Last year we had a girl come in to get a blood test for her marriage license, and we had to stick her six times in four places before we got anything."

"Yes, I know," I said. "That was me!"

—CONNIE DOWN

A man is recovering from minor surgery when his nurse comes in to check on him.
"How are you feeling?" she asks.
"I'm okay," he says, "but I didn't like the four-letter word the doctor used during surgery."
"What did he say?" the nurse asks.

"Oops."

—ROBERT REA

While attending a convention, three psychiatrists take a walk. "People are always coming to us with their guilt and fears," one says, "but we have no one to go to with our own problems."

"Since we're all professionals," another suggests, "why don't we hear each other out right now?" They agree this is a good idea.

The first psychiatrist confesses, "I'm a compulsive shopper and deeply in debt, so I overbill patients as often as I can."

The second admits, "I have a drug problem that's out of control, and I frequently pressure my patients into buying illegal drugs for me."

The third psychiatrist says, "I know it's wrong, but no matter how hard I try, I just can't keep a secret."

—AMY BERTMAN

I was at a sporting event when a gentleman behind me gasped and fell over. I climbed over the seat and first established that he was breathing. As I checked the man's pulse rhythm, a woman stormed over and pushed me away.

"Step aside! I'm a nurse!" she shouted. She then proceeded to examine the man.

As I retreated to my seat, I announced, "When you get to the part about 'Call a doctor,' I'll be here."

—KARL J. PIZZOLATTO, MD

Helen goes to a psychiatrist and says, "Doctor, you've got to do something about my husband—he thinks he's a refrigerator!"

"I wouldn't worry too much about it," the shrink replies. "Lots of people have harmless delusions. It will pass."

"But, Doctor, you don't understand," Helen insists. "He sleeps with his mouth open, and the little light keeps me awake."

—JOHN R. LOPEZ, JR.

Shorthand is the norm in the medical field when taking notes. For example, HTN stands for "hypertension." I did a double take, though, when a diabetic patient came into the ER suffering from high blood sugar levels. The nurse had charted the complaint as "Out of control BS."

—SHERRELL LAM

As my friend, an anesthesiologist at a hospital, passed by an operating room, she noticed it was being set up for a breast augmentation procedure. So she popped her head inside.

"What's going on?" she asked a nurse.

The nurse's reply: "They're making a mountain out of a molehill."

—YO KLEIN

My doctor told me to stop having intimate dinners for four. Unless there are three other people.

—ORSON WELLES

A man was very skeptical of chiropractors, but when no other treatment seemed to relieve the chronic pain in his back, he decided to give it a try. Before his first appointment, he told the chiropractor of his reservations, but after a few adjustments, he felt better than he had in years.

"What do you think now?" the chiropractor asked.

"Well," the man replied, "I guess I stand corrected."

—CHRIS J. DEIGHAN

Doctor, Doctor

. . . I keep having déjà vu.
Doc: Didn't I see you yesterday?

. . . my son swallowed a roll of film.
Doc: Let's wait and see what develops.

Our nine-year-old son had hurt his leg, and my husband, an automobile engineer, took him to the family doctor. "Please repair him," my husband said to the doctor. Then realizing he hadn't used the right words, he tried again, "I mean, fix him right . . . I mean, do whatever you like to call it, but put him back on the road!"

—BELA AGARWAL

Although my doctor stopped by my hospital room to see me every day while I was recuperating from an operation, he hardly said two words to me. But once, after being unusually chatty, he remarked, "It sure has been nice talking to you. All my other patients are in comas."

—LILLIAN B. MCDADE

The doctor was trying to encourage a gloomy patient.

"You're in no real danger," he said. "Why, I've had the same complaint myself."

"Yes," the patient moaned, "but you didn't have the same doctor!"

—LILLIAN M. DECKER

After a checkup, a doctor asked his patient, "Is there anything you'd like to discuss?"

"Well," said the patient, "I was thinking about getting a vasectomy."

"That's a big decision. Have you talked it over with your family?"

"Yes, we took a vote . . . and they're in favor of it 15 to 2."

Waiting in the ER for test results, I overheard a doctor talking to another patient. "So," he said, "I understand you've lost the ability to speak. When did this happen?"

—ANNA GOODBERLET

As a student nurse, I had to give an injection to a 79-year-old male patient. I asked which hip he preferred the shot in. He wanted to know if he really had a choice. I told him he did. He looked me straight in the eye and said, "yours!"

—KAY NYLAND

Why is a hospital gown like health insurance?

You're never as covered as you think you are.

Joe was suffering from excruciating headaches. The doctor told him he could cure the headaches, but it would require castration. "You have a rare condition that causes pressure to build up against your spine," the doctor explained. "This, in turn, causes headaches. The only cure is surgery." Joe was shocked but had the operation.

When he left the hospital, Joe was depressed, so he stopped at a men's shop for a new suit. The salesman eyed him and said, "44 long?"

"That's right," Joe said. He tried on the suit, and it fit perfectly.

"How about a new shirt?" the salesman asked. "Let's see, a 34 sleeve and 16½ neck ought to do it."

"Right again," Joe said. "You're simply amazing."

"While we're at it, how about some new underwear?" the salesman suggested. He eyed Joe's waist and said, "Size 36."

"Nope, you finally missed one," Joe said, chuckling. "I wear size 34."

"You couldn't possibly," replied the salesman. "Underwear that tight would create a great deal of pressure against your spine and cause one heck of a headache."

—BRYAN ELDRING

❝ I suggest you just call yourself a white horse with black stripes and avoid years of expensive therapy. ❞

While my friend Cheryl was working as a receptionist for an eye surgeon, a very angry woman stormed up to her desk.

"Someone stole my wig while I was having surgery yesterday," she complained. The doctor came out and tried to calm her down.

"I assure you no one on my staff would have done such a thing," he said. "Why do you think it was taken here?"

"After the operation, I noticed the wig I had on was ugly and cheap-looking."

"I think," explained the surgeon gently, "that means your cataract operation was a success."

—RAHEELA A. SHAIKH

A doctor was addressing a large audience in the Grange Hall.

"The material we put into our stomachs is enough to have killed most of us sitting here years ago. Red meat is awful. Soft drinks corrode your stomach lining. High-fat diets can be dangerous. But there is one food that causes the most grief and suffering for years after eating it. Can anyone tell me what that is?"

After several seconds of quiet, a 75-year-old man in the front row raised his hand and softly said, "Wedding cake."

—CHARLES NICKEL LACEY

John tells his shrink, "Last night I dreamed you were my mother."

"How do you feel about that?" asks the psychiatrist.

"I haven't had time to think about it," says John. "I overslept this morning. Then I remembered I had an appointment with you, so I gobbled down a Coke and a cookie and came straight here."

"A Coke and a cookie?" the doc replies. "You call that breakfast?"

A young doctor friend, a newcomer to Maine, reported that the famous New England reticence was more powerful even than he had anticipated. Called to the home of an elderly woman who had pneumonia, he asked her if she had ever had penicillin. "Oh, yes," she replied. Thus reassured, he gave her a shot. Later that night, his patient was admitted to the hospital with a severe penicillin reaction. After several hours, the danger passed. Standing at the patient's bedside, our relieved friend was discussing with another doctor the sheer bad luck of encountering such a major reaction in one who had taken the drug before.

Suddenly the patient interrupted him. "Now, Doctor, you don't need to feel bad about this. Why, the last time I had a penicillin shot, the very same thing happened."

—JANE HUNT

Patient: Lately I feel that everyone takes advantage of me.
Psychiatrist: Don't worry about it. That's perfectly normal.
Patient: Really? Thanks a lot, Doc. How much do I owe you?
Psychiatrist: How much do you have?

—TOM MCQUEEN

Looking down at his patient, the doctor decided to tell him the truth: "I feel I should tell you that you are a very sick man. The situation is complex and confusing, and things don't look too promising. Now, is there anyone you would like to see?" Bending down toward the man, the doctor heard a feeble yes. "Who is it?" asked the doctor. In a slightly stronger tone, the sufferer said, "Another doctor."

—CHARLES WADSWORTH

DIVINE LAUGHTER

My teenage daughter is not the most knowledgeable Catholic. After my husband bought me a gorgeous cross pendant, Michelle gushed, "It looks like something the Pope's wife would wear!"

—BECKY O'NEILL

When my elderly friend told me about a lesbian she knew and how wonderful she thought she was, I figured it was the perfect time to fess up to her.

"You know, I'm a lesbian too," I said. "And so is the gal I live with."

"I didn't know that," she said, and then, shrugging, added, "but everyone has a right to their own religion."

—DIANE ROBINETTE

Why there aren't church hecklers.

When my brother was a pastor in Thunder Bay, he usually put the title of his upcoming sermons on a street-side bulletin board. One week, his sermon was "Hell, the Forgotten Horror." Underneath was the permanent message printed at the bottom of the sign: "A Warm Welcome to All."

—JUDY MAJOR

As our priest went along the line of worshippers, giving them Holy Communion, he saw what he thought was a communion wafer lying on the floor. Because, as blessed bread, it had to be consumed, he popped it into his mouth.

"Mummy, Mummy," the small boy next to me cried out. "The vicar's eaten my *Save the Children* badge."

—PAM DAVIES

The high school was using our church's Family Life Center for its annual spring banquet. Since we wanted to keep the teenagers confined to the gym and out of the main building, someone suggested posting a Do Not Enter sign on the door. I knew that wouldn't work, so I put up another sign that did the job. It read, Prayer Room.

—BILL DENHAM

A businessman who needed millions of dollars to clinch an important deal went to church to pray for the money. By chance he knelt next to a man who was praying for $100 to pay an urgent debt. The businessman took out his wallet and pressed $100 into the other man's hand. Overjoyed, the man got up and left the church. The businessman then closed his eyes and prayed, "And now, Lord, that I have your undivided attention . . ."

—BRENDAN P. EDET

As church secretary, I prepare the bulletin for each week's services. One Sunday morning, I heard snickering from the pews. Quickly grabbing the bulletin, I found the cause. The sermon title for that day was: **"What Makes God Sick: Pastor Joe Smith."**

—DEANNE BLAND

Spotted on a church marquee: **"Love your enemies; After all, you made them."**

—BARBARA TELECSAN

A doctor, an engineer and a lawyer were arguing over whose profession was the oldest.

"On the sixth day, God took one of Adam's ribs and created Eve," said the doctor. "So that makes him a surgeon first."

"Please," said the engineer. "Before that, God created the world from chaos and confusion, so he was first an engineer."

"Interesting," said the lawyer smugly, "but who do you think created the chaos and confusion?"

—LYNDELL LEATHERMAN

It was Easter Sunday at our military chapel. The pastor called the children to the front and told them the story of how Jesus was crucified by the Romans, his body placed in a tomb and the front covered by a stone.

"But on the third day," he said, "the stone was rolled away, and Jesus was not there. Do you know what happened next?"

One kid shouted, "Jesus turned into a zombie and went after the Romans!"

—LOU DELTUFO

At a church social one evening, as the secretary's husband served me a cup of coffee, I noticed a nasty-looking purplish bruise under one of his fingernails. "Dave," I asked teasingly, "just what did you say when that happened?"

"Hoover," he answered.

"Hoover?" I repeated.

"Yes," he said. "That was the biggest dam I could think of."

—NOREEN WEBSTER

"I need to speak to you about these emoticons you keep slipping into the scriptures."

One Sunday my teenage son was in church. When the collection plate was passed around, he pulled a dollar bill from his pocket and dropped it in.

Just at that moment, the person behind him tapped him on the shoulder and handed him a $20 bill. Secretly admiring the man's generosity, my son placed the $20 in the plate and passed it on. Then he felt another tap from behind and heard a whisper: "Son, that was your $20. It fell out of your pocket."

—MARY C. LOWE

In my role as a pastor of a Baptist church, I visited a woman with a bad back. She was down on the floor, the most comfortable position she could find. I asked if she would like me to lay my hands on her back and pray, to which she said "yes."

I quickly felt a significant surge of warmth from her back, and I excitedly explained that this could be God performing the healing process.

"I'm sorry to disappoint you," she said, "but that is my hot water bottle."

—DAVID HILL

By the time the morning service was to begin, only one man was in the church. The minister said to him, "It looks like everyone has slept in. Do you want to go home or should I preach the sermon?"

The man replied, "When I go to feed the chickens and only one comes, I still feed it."

The minister took that as a yes, mounted the pulpit and delivered an hour-long sermon. At the end, he asked the man what he thought. His answer: "When I go to feed the chickens and only one comes, I don't give it the whole bucket!"

—RENEE DAGG

A young boy arrived late to his Sunday school class. He was normally punctual so the teacher asked him if anything was wrong.

"No," said the boy. "I had planned to go fishing, but my father told me that I had to go to church instead."

Impressed, the teacher asked the boy if his father had explained why it was more important to go to church than to go fishing.

"Yes," the boy replied. "He said he didn't have enough bait for both of us."

—CHAU PEI YING

Many years ago, we had a beloved archdeacon in our parish church. His wife was very supportive and sometimes, when he was preaching from the pulpit, she would hand him a note. It might have been about a thought that had just occurred to her or something she wanted to make sure he hadn't forgotten. He would often read these notes to the congregation.

I remember one Sunday when the rector read the note his wife had just handed to him: "Dear, your wig is crooked."

—ALBERT JAMES

After 48 years in the priesthood our elderly parish priest was due to retire.

Throughout the months leading up to his retirement there were celebrations at the church as well as at the elementary school where my children were in attendance.

On the Sunday of Father's second last Mass my nine-year-old daughter, Meagan, whispered to me, "Father must be getting really excited."

"Why?" I asked.

"Because NOW he can get married!" Meagan replied.

—ELAINE KIRBYSON

Sam shows up at a revival meeting, seeking help.

"I need you to pray for my hearing," he tells the preacher.

The preacher puts his fingers on Sam's ears and prays and prays. When he's done, he asks, "How's your hearing now?"

"I don't know," says Sam. **"I don't go to court till next Tuesday."**

—JAMES HOSKIN

A woman I know quite well told me outside church, "I'm ashamed to admit it, but I can never remember your husband's name."

"It's Neville," I said, adding jokingly, "just remember it rhymes with devil."

The next time we met, she called, "Good morning, Nathan."

"Where did you get Nathan from?" I asked, bemused.

"You told me it rhymed with Satan," she replied.

—JANE DAVIS

My husband, who is a pastor, was having a conversation with our children about the differences between religions.

My daughter, Sarah, wanted to know the differences between a Roman Catholic priest and a minister. He explained that one of the biggest differences is that priests do not marry. My husband also said that a priest devotes his life to God, and that marriage and a family would distract him from his duties. But a pastor, who also dedicates his life to serve God, can marry. "It's like having your cake and eating it too," he said.

Sarah's response: "Priests can't eat cake?"

—JO-ANNE TWINEM

Spotted in my church bulletin: **"The church will host an evening of fine dining, super entertainment and gracious hostility."**

—SHARON OWEN

Two old friends, Quinn, a Christian, and Sophie, a Jew, are having lunch when Sophie says to her friend, "Don't take this personally, but how can you honestly believe that Jesus walked on water, turned water into wine or made the infirm walk?"

"Well, look at it this way," says Quinn, "maybe there were rocks beneath the water's surface, and he crossed over them. Or maybe there was a little wine in the water, and that's what someone tasted. As for healing the sick, maybe they just needed his guidance. But who are you to question my beliefs? What about Moses parting the Red Sea?"

Sophie nods thoughtfully. "Wasn't that something?"

—PATTI BROWNE

An angel appears at a faculty meeting and tells the dean, "In return for your unselfish and exemplary behavior, the Lord will reward you with your choice of infinite wealth, wisdom or beauty."

"Give me infinite wisdom!" declares the dean, without hesitation.

"Done!" says the angel before disappearing in a cloud of smoke.

All heads now turn to the dean, who sits surrounded by a faint halo of light. "Well," says a colleague, "say something brilliant."

The dean stands and, with the poise of Socrates, opines, "I should have taken the money."

—HENRY MIXON

"Not another Powerpoint sermon!"

Once a year our church group holds a sale to raise money for its youth group. At our last sale, just as we finished putting everything out, a middle-aged man arrived in a huff. Growling, he yanked two sports coats and a few suits off the clothes rack, then stomped over to the cash, where a puzzled volunteer asked if everything was all right.

"I don't know what the world is coming to," the man said in an injured tone. "This is the third year my wife's given my favorite clothes to this church sale!"

—MAGGIE THEISS

Shortly after the evening service at my local church began, there was a torrential downpour.

After the rain stopped, I heard the persistent drip of water as it trickled through the roof.

This was very distracting, and at the end of the service I told the minister: "I have just spent the evening listening to the most annoying drip I've ever heard!"

I only realized what I had said when I saw the shock on the minister's face.

—ISHBEL MACKAY

My church choir was in the middle of rehearsing a requiem for an upcoming concert and, with the concert date fast approaching, our director was getting a little more picky about various elements of our performance. During one rehearsal he interrupted us to comment on the fact that we were breathing in the wrong spot.

"No, no, no!" he said. **"There is to be no breathing after death."**

—TRACY BAXTER

An elderly Frenchman is in his local church's confessional.

"Forgive me Father, for I have sinned," he says. "During the Second World War a beautiful woman knocked on my door and asked me to hide her from the enemy. I put her in the attic."

"No need to ask forgiveness for that, my son," says the priest. "It was a wonderful thing to do."

"Yeah," says the man, "But she started offering me sexual favors in return, and I went along with it."

"People in wartime situations do funny things. If you are truly sorry for your actions, you are forgiven."

"That's a great load off my mind," says the pensioner. "May I ask you a question?"

"Of course."

"She's getting on a bit now. Should I tell her the war is over?"

—WAYNE EVANS

One night, the lights went out in the church I used to attend right when the minister was reading the Bible. He then recommended that those present pray in silence until the situation was resolved.

Among the faithful was an elderly gentleman who slept regularly during service. In this precise moment of silence and darkness, he woke up and yelled, "Damn them all! They went away and left me here alone!"

—SAMUEL SCHULKA

A few years ago, I successfully completed the process and was about to be ordained as a pastor in our church. We shared this joyous news with my mother-in-law who took great pride telling her friends.

We laughed, however, when we heard what she was saying to them: "Bob is being pasteurized."

—BOB BADDELEY

After a frustrating morning of getting our four children packed up and off to church, we attempted to get everybody into the front pew with minimal disruption.
We were sitting down when the pastor mentioned a scripture that said children were a blessing, like a quiver full of arrows.

"Yeah," my wife replied,

"Sometimes I just can't wait to shoot them."

—THOMAS ZIMMERMANN

Our new minister pleaded with the congregation for help on a church project. After weeks with few takers, he called our house with this deeply felt, if not diplomatic, request: "I am scraping the bottom of the barrel for volunteers and wonder if you might be able to help?"

—VIRGINIA NIFONG

A young parish minister about to deliver his first sermon asked a retired cleric for advice on how to capture the congregation's attention.

"Start with an opening line that's certain to grab them," the older man said. "For example: 'Some of the best years of my life were spent in the arms of a woman who was not my wife.'" He smiled at the younger man's shocked expression before adding, "She was my mother."

The next Sunday, the young clergyman nervously clutched the pulpit rail in front of the congregation. Finally he said, "Some of the best years of my life were spent in the arms of a woman." He was pleased at the instant reaction—then became panic-stricken. "But for the life of me, I can't remember who she was!"

—GIL HARRIS

QUOTABLE QUOTES

"How can I believe in God when just last week I got my tongue caught in the roller of an electric typewriter?"

—WOODY ALLEN

"IF THERE IS NO GOD, WHO POPS UP THE NEXT KLEENEX?"

—ART HOPPE

"They say such nice things about people at their funerals that it makes me sad that I'm going to miss mine by just a few days."

—GARRISON KEILLOR

"The secret to a good sermon is to have a good beginning and a good ending, then having the two as close together as possible."

—GEORGE BURNS

"CLOUD NINE GETS ALL THE PUBLICITY, BUT CLOUD EIGHT ACTUALLY IS CHEAPER, LESS CROWDED AND HAS A BETTER VIEW."

—GEORGE CARLIN

"To lose one parent may be regarded as a misfortune; to lose both looks like carelessness".

—OSCAR WILDE

"I DON'T PRAY BECAUSE I DON'T WANT TO BORE GOD."

—ORSON WELLES

"When did I realize I was God? Well, I was praying, and I suddenly realized I was talking to myself."

—PETER O'TOOLE

"What I look forward to is continued immaturity followed by death."

—DAVE BARRY

"According to our records, you once Googled God's name in vain."

PASSING ON

Carl and Abe are two old baseball fanatics. They agree that whoever dies first will try to come back and tell the other one if there's baseball in heaven.

One evening, Abe passes away in his sleep. A few nights later, Carl hears what sounds like Abe's voice. "Abe, is that you?" he asks.

"Of course it's me," Abe replies.

"I can't believe it," Carl whispers. "So tell me, is there baseball in heaven?"

"Well, I have good news and bad news," Abe says. "The good news is, yes, there's baseball in heaven. The bad news is you're pitching tomorrow night!"

—DAVID DANGLER

An old lady visits her recently deceased husband at the funeral parlor. When she sees him, she starts crying.

"He's wearing a black suit," she tells the undertaker. "It was his dying wish to be buried in blue."

The undertaker apologizes, saying that it's normal practice to put bodies in a black suit, but he'll see what he can arrange.

Next day, the woman returns and there is her husband resplendent in a blue suit. "That's wonderful," she says. "Where did you get it?"

"Well," explains the undertaker, "After you left, a man about your husband's size was brought in wearing a blue suit. His wife said that he wanted to be buried in black and was there anything we could do?"

The old lady smiles at the undertaker.

"After that," he continues, "It was simply a matter of swapping the heads."

—ROBERT A'COURT

The flyer invited me to a seminar entitled: **"Everything You Ever Wanted to Ask About Cremation." The location: Smokehouse BBQ.**

—L.J.

My wife's mother had a great sense of humor and was "Grama" to everyone in our extended family. When she died at 87 after a lingering illness, three generations of the family gathered at the funeral home.

When the visitors had left, my wife approached the casket with three of our grandchildren and told them that they could touch Grama if they wished.

The two older children timidly touched Grama's arm and quickly pulled away. But when two-year-old Keiran was lifted up, she firmly placed both hands on Grama and declared, "Yup, she's dead all right!"

Grama would have just loved it.

—PERCY AFFLECK

Sue passed away, so her husband, Bubba, called 911. The operator said they'd send someone out right away. "Where do you live?" asked the operator.

Bubba replied, "At the end of Eucalyptus Drive."

The operator asked, "Can you spell that for me?"

There was a long pause. Finally Bubba said, "How 'bout if I drag her over to Oak Street, and you pick her up there?"

On our way to a funeral home for the viewing of a friend's father, I reminded my three-year-old daughter to be quiet and respectful. And she was—right up to the end, when she asked, "Mommy, who's the man in the treasure chest?"

—JENNIFER TURK

As an Anglican priest, I was asked one Sunday to inter the ashes of an elderly couple who had died just weeks apart. The service was held in a small, rural cemetery that I wasn't familiar with, so after the service, I wandered around, looking at headstones. Most carried the usual epitaphs: "Safe in the arms of Jesus," "At rest." One stood out, though. Its message: "This was not my idea!"

—REV. KEN BOND

Patrons of a pub mourned the passing of the bar's mutt, Spot. They cut off his tail and framed it as a memorial. Spot was about to enter heaven when St. Peter stopped him. "Heaven's a place of perfection," said the saint. "You deserve to enter, but not without your tail. Go back and retrieve it."

In the middle of the night, Spot scratched on the door of the pub.

"It's the spirit of our dear Spot!" exclaimed the bartender. "What can I do for you?"

Spot said he needed his tail to enter heaven.

"Oh, sorry," the barkeeper replied, "but my liquor license doesn't allow me to retail spirits after hours."

—CRAIG IAN DUFT

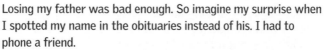

Losing my father was bad enough. So imagine my surprise when I spotted my name in the obituaries instead of his. I had to phone a friend.

"Did you see the report of my death in the paper?" I asked.

"Yes," he said. **"Where are you calling from?"**

—RALPH WARTH

"I'm afraid of the dark, so could I get one with a night light?"

A man walked into a bar and saw an old friend dejectedly nursing a drink. "You look terrible," the man said.

"My mother died in March and left me $10,000," the friend replied. "Then in April my father died and left me $20,000."

"Gee, that's tough, losing both parents in two months."

"Then to top it off," the friend said, "my aunt died last month and left me $50,000."

"How sad."

"Tell me about it," the friend continued. "So far this month, nothing."

—RACHEL SIDELL

A preacher was contacted by the local funeral director to hold a graveside service for someone with no family or friends. The preacher started out early for the cemetery but quickly got lost, making several wrong turns.

He arrived a half hour late, and the hearse was nowhere in sight. Seeing some workmen eating lunch, the preacher went to the open grave nearby and found the casket already in the ground. Taking out his prayer book, he read the service.

As he was returning to his car, he overheard one workman ask another: "Should we tell him it's a septic tank?"

—COLIN ENGLISH

I accidentally rear-ended a car while driving our funeral home van. The couple was unhurt, but the driver seemed shaken. When we exchanged information, I remarked that her name sounded familiar. "That's because we made our funeral arrangements with you six months ago," she said, "but we never thought you'd come looking for us!"

—DAVID K. SHEWCHUK

A teacher, a petty thief and a lawyer all died and went to the Pearly Gates. Because of crowding, St. Peter told them they had to pass a test before ascending any further. Addressing the teacher, he asked, "What was the name of the famous ship that hit an iceberg and sank?"

"The Titanic," she answered, and St. Peter motioned her into heaven.

The thief was next. "How many people died on that ship?" St. Peter asked.

"Gee, that's tough," the man replied. "But luckily I just saw the movie. The answer is 1500." St. Peter let him through.

Then St. Peter turned to the lawyer. "Name them."

—LYNDELL LEATHERMAN

One of the deceased at our funeral home was a farmer who had suffered a heart attack while helping a cow in labor. The headline on his obituary read **"Mr. Jones Dies While Giving Birth to a Calf."**

—DEBORAH HUDSON

A man died and went to hell. As he passed sulfurous pits and shrieking sinners, he saw his town's most notorious lawyer snuggling up to a beautiful model. "This is so unfair," the man bellowed to the devil. "I have to roast and suffer for all eternity, and that sleazy lawyer gets to spend it with her?"

"Silence!" the devil demanded, jabbing his trident at the man. "You must pay your penance, and the model must pay hers!"

—ANGELA M. SALIANI

I sat down at the computer to prepare the order of service for my much-loved uncle's funeral. After the opening prayers came the first hymn. As I typed in, "Dear Lord and Father of Mankind," the little computer man on Microsoft Word popped up: "It looks like you're writing a letter. Would you like help?"

—LYN MCCULLOCH

While my parents were making their funeral arrangements, the cemetery salesman pointed out a plot that he thought they would like. "You'll have a beautiful view of the swan pond," he assured them.

Dad wasn't sold: "Unless you're including a periscope with my casket, I don't know how I'm going to enjoy it."

—CAROL BEACH

A few weeks after the death of my father-in-law, I found my seven-year-old son crying in bed. His grandmother had died the previous year, and he was taking it all very hard.

"You know, Kyle," I said, "when we die, we'll get to see Grandma and Grandpa again in heaven."

With tears spilling down his face, Kyle cried, "That's easy for you to say. You don't have that long!"

—FARREL CHAPMAN

On the way to the funeral home to confirm arrangements for my mother's funeral, my dad, my sister and I were trying to decide on appropriate music for the visitation. Dad said that Mom loved the Bee Gees, so I said we could have their music playing softly in the background.

Laughing, my sister said, "I think we should skip 'Stayin' Alive.'"

—KAREN HOLTZ

An undertaker friend organized the funeral of a man who was to be buried on his birthday. To mark the sad irony, the man's young grandson asked if he could put a card in the coffin.

My friend happily agreed—not realizing it was a musical card. As the coffin was carried through the church, the movement knocked the card off the departed's chest and triggered its mechanism.

The service remained dignified, but its solemnity was somewhat undermined by a tinny voice singing "Happy birthday to you, happy birthday to you" from somewhere inside the coffin.

—ALAN HASKEY

In hell, you have to find the start to Scotch tape over and over.

—MOLLY_KATS, ON TWITTER

As director of a small funeral home I handle most functions, including answering the telephone. One day, I picked up the phone and said: "Funeral services. This is Wayne speaking. How may I help you?"

"I think I have the wrong number," the woman replied. "I was calling a travel agency, but I don't want to go where you'd send me!"

—WAYNE BOYLAN

My mom was telling me about her prearranged funeral and about the urn she chose, which cost more than the cremation itself. She described it in great detail, then added,

"Wait 'til you see me in it!"

—KATHY SMITH

On returning home from a funeral, I told my daughter and son-in-law that I didn't want a service when I died, just a tea. "A nice tea," I added.

There was a pause, then my son-in-law piped up, "Would it be possible for you to do some baking and put it in the freezer?"

—FLOSS THOMSON

Lying on his deathbed, a loving husband was wavering between life and death when he thought he smelled chocolate chip cookies baking. They were his favorite, so he dragged himself out of bed, crawled to the kitchen and was just reaching up to take a cookie off the plate when his wife slapped his hand with a spatula.

"Don't touch!" she commanded. "They're for the funeral."

—COLIN TAYLOR

When my quiet grandfather, Jack, passed away, my family gathered at the funeral parlor to pay their respects. Since we are a large family spread out over much of the continent, the atmosphere became quite festive as family members reunited. My grandmother, who always loved a party, could not help but comment: "Well, isn't this just like old times; we're all here having a great time, and there's Jack, over in the corner, not saying a word!"

—DARREN WHITE

I was passing a funeral parlor with my four-year-old daughter just as the hearse pulled in.

"What's that funny-looking car?" she asked.

"It's used to take dead people to the cemetery," I explained.

She glanced at the driver and his stern-looking assistant dressed in black and replied, "Oh, yes, I can see one sitting in the front."

—SUSAN FITCH

You'd die of embarrassment if these phrases appeared in your obituary:

- "She leaves behind a brother and 117 cats."
- "Passed away in a failed stunt that has already been viewed more than 40 million times on YouTube."
- "Was always quick to point out others' grammatical errors."
- "Survived by his parents and his animatronic wife, Elizabot."

—CHRIS WHITE

My husband, a funeral director, was at work one day when our daughter, Patricia, was in a car accident. Coming out of shock, Patricia found a woman hovering over her.

"Is there anything I can do?" the woman asked.

"Call Anderson's Funeral Home," Patricia moaned.

The woman looked surprised. "Oh, you'll be all right, dear," she reassured her.

—KAY ANDERSON

JUST
for
LAUGHS

"The world has always been fragile. Just ask the dinosaurs."

—MICHAEL SHANNON

HUMOR IN UNIFORM

Soon after being transferred to a new duty station, my marine husband called home one evening to tell me he would be late. "Dirty magazines were discovered in the platoon quarters," he said, "and the whole squad is being disciplined."

I launched into a tirade, arguing that marines should not be penalized for something so trivial.

My husband interrupted. "Honey, when I said 'dirty magazines,' I meant the clips from their rifles hadn't been cleaned."

—MILLIE COURTIS

A navy man and new to town, I found a barbershop with a sign in the window that read "Military Cuts Our Specialty."

I walked in and told the barber exactly what I wanted: "A standard Naval Aviator. Do you know what that is?"

"Sure," he said. "Blocked in the back, 2.5 inches on the sides, and you expect me to make you better-looking than you actually are."

—CHRIS FARRINGTON

My brother was vacationing on a beach when he heard someone call to him using an old nickname from his navy days. My brother couldn't place the face, but the man insisted they had served together, and he even told stories of their days on the high seas.

Soon the memories came flooding back. As they reminisced, the friend revealed that he had received a medical discharge.

"What was wrong?" my brother asked.

His friend replied dolefully, "The doctor said that I suffer from amnesia."

—RUTH FALCÃO

Home on leave from Iraq, my step-grandson was showing off his abs. Not to be outdone, my husband thumped his prodigious stomach and bragged, "I still have my six-pack. It's just six inches deeper."

—K.H.

On his first day of army basic training, my husband stood with the other recruits as the sergeant asked, "How many of you are smokers?"

Several men raised their hands.

"Congratulations!" he said. "You just quit."

—CHRISTINA KOSATKA

When I invited an army friend to a party, I offered to give him directions. He declined, saying, "I've invaded three countries in five years. I think I can find your house."

—RITA BRISTOL

I taught a class on human relations to basic trainees, where we discussed how everyone deserves respect. At the end of one class, their training instructor stuck his head in and shouted, "Okay, you babies, let's get out of here. We have places to go!"

As he passed me, an airman mumbled, "Now back to reality."

—PAT FERRY

A sign your child has been raised in a military family: My daughter was playing with Barbie dolls. Seeing a lone Ken doll among all those women, I said, "Poor Ken, he's the only guy."

"Yeah," she said. "All the rest of the dads are deployed."

—MELINDA KUNZ

Have you heard of World War II?" my husband asked our six-year-old grandson.

"Well, I've heard of it," Bronson said tentatively. "But I can't remember what game it is."

—LORNA PACKARD

"You have four cavities!" barked the naval dentist, looking at my X-rays. He grabbed a huge steel syringe and shot both sides of my mouth full of novocaine. He then looked at the X-rays and then my mouth. Then back at the X-rays and again at my mouth. Then he sat down.

"I have good news and bad news," he said. "The bad news is, these are not your X-rays. The good news is, you're cured."

—PAUL STANIC

During Operation Iraqi Freedom, the marines in my squadron went out of their way to make themselves feel at home. In front of the trailers that served as our administrative offices, the gravel front "lawn" was carefully groomed and lined with a border of sandbags. In the center was a wooden sign: "Keep Off the Grass!"

—BETHANY KOSHUTA

On my grandfather's first day of boot camp, his drill sergeant brought the unit to attention and asked, "Is anyone here musically inclined?"

Seeing an easy job in the offing, three soldiers, including Grandpa, raised their hands.

"Good," said the sergeant. "You three will move the commander's piano."

—BRANT DEICHMANN

Being color-blind excluded me from certain jobs in the marines. But my recruiter took pity on me and gave me a color vision test book to memorize before taking the eye test. Later that week, I took the test and successfully recited each color in the book. The doctor was impressed.

"Excellent," he said. "Just one thing: I opened the book on page two."

—DAN KEHL

My sister had her kindergarten class write to my nephew Nate and his marine buddies serving in Afghanistan. Nate's favorite letter was this one: **"Dear Marine, thank you for being in the army."**

—ANNE KOPP

In Iraq, my sergeant was not happy with the speed with which I was moving MREs (Meals Ready to Eat) from a non-air-conditioned building into an air-conditioned tent.

"Hurry up," he yelled. "The sun's going to ruin those MREs. Have you ever had a bad MRE?"

Moving a pallet, I grunted, "You ever had a good one?"

—CHRIS NEWTON

" Before we launch an attack, let's make sure we unfriend them first. "

I took my four-year-old great-grandson to the Leavenworth
National Cemetery, where my husband is buried.
While there, we heard the sound of a bugle.

"What's that?" asked Jeremiah.

"'Taps.' They play it at a soldier's burial," I explained.

A minute later came the honorary rifle salute.
With eyes bugging out, Jeremiah asked,

"Did they shoot him?!?"

—JACKI CAHILL

After a snowstorm buried our neighborhood, my wife called
the hospital and said she could not make it to work because all the
roads were blocked.

"We'll send the National Guard," she was told. "They'll get
you out."

"Good luck with that," she said. "My husband's in the National
Guard, and he can't get out either."

—BRIAN WOOLSHLEGER

On the first morning of boot camp, our unit was dragged out
of bed by our drill sergeant and made to assemble outside. "My
name is Sergeant Jackson," he snarled. "Is there anyone here who
thinks he can whip me?"

My six-foot-three, 280-pound brother, who had enlisted with
me, raised his hand. "Yes, sir, I do."

Our sergeant grabbed him by the arm and led him out in front
of the group. "Men," he said, "this is my new assistant. Now, is
there anyone here who thinks he can whip both of us?"

—ROBERT NORRIS

As we set out on patrol in Afghanistan, my platoon leader was torn between which route to take.

"One road will probably get us ambushed," he said. "But if we take the second, we'll likely run into IEDs. What do you think?"

I considered our options, then gave him my suggestion: **"I say we take a couple of days off."**

—RYAN HENDRICKS

As a dental officer in the air force, I was treating a recruit. As he lay prone in the chair, I asked him a question about his pain level. He responded, "Yes."

"Yes is not enough," I said.

With that, he leaped out of the chair, stood at attention and shouted, "Yes, sir!"

—DOUGLAS C. BOYD, DMD

With the help of a balky 16-ton forklift, I was loading containers onto an aircraft bound for Afghanistan. Our sergeant major stopped by to ask how I was doing.

"It would be easier if the idiot who owns the red truck would move it," I complained.

"Okay," he replied. "I will."

—CPL. DEBBIE MACNEIL

A sergeant was trying to sell us new soldiers on the idea of joining the airborne division. His pitch clearly needed work.

"The first week, we separate the men from the boys," he began. "The second week, we separate the men from the idiots. The third week, the idiots jump."

—JIMMY RONEY

While standing watch in the coast guard station in Juneau, Alaska, I got a call from the navy. They had lost contact with one of their planes and needed us to send an aircraft to find it. I asked the man where the plane had last been spotted so we would know where to search.

"I can't tell you," he said. "That's classified."

—ALFRED MILES

My son, stationed in Japan, dated a Japanese girl who spoke little English. That didn't faze him until the night she announced, "I have chicken pox."

My son didn't know whether to run or get her to the hospital. Then he noticed her shiver.

"You don't have chicken pox," he said. "You have goose bumps."

—NEJLA WILLIAMS BODINE

During inspection, a female officer asked our very nervous corporal what his first general order was.

"Sir, this cadet's first general order is to take charge of this post and all government property in view, sir!"

Excellent response, except for one detail.

"Do I look like a ma'am or a sir?" the officer demanded.

The startled corporal bellowed back, "Sir, you're a ma'am, sir!"

—MATT WAKEFIELD

Overheard: Two veterans chatting about the Korean War.

First Guy: What knife did you use over there?

Second Guy: I didn't have a knife. I figured that if I needed to use it, I was too close to the enemy.

—KAITLYN WILDE

When a coworker from my old firm was deployed abroad, the boss placed this sticky note on his door: "Stepped out. Back in 12 months."

—JOYCE HUANG

The five-year-old boy at our school was from a military family: His mother was a fighter pilot, and his father served in Afghanistan.

"Do you know my full name?" he asked me.

"No, I don't," I said.

"It's James Phillip Thomas Steven Harold Jackson the Third. But my mother calls me Steven. My father's full name is James Phillip Thomas Steven Harold Jackson the Second."

"And what does your mother call him?"

"Cupcake."

—M. JACKSON

When my very pregnant niece, a sergeant in the New York Army National Guard, accidentally knocked over a glass of water, one of her soldiers volunteered to help clean it up. As he was mopping up the mess, an officer walked in.

"Private, what's going on in here?" he asked.

To the officer's horror, the private replied, "Sir, the sergeant's water broke, and I'm helping her clean up."

—DAVID HEATON

During my time in the navy, everyone was getting KP or guard duty except me. Not wanting to get in trouble, I asked the ensign why.

"What's your name?" he asked.

"Michael Zyvoloski."

"That's why. I can't pronounce it, much less spell it."

—MICHAEL J. ZYVOLOSKI

"The war games are going well, sir.
We've just reached level four, where our M-16s turn
into fire-breathing, tank-eating dragons."

My boot camp platoon was last in line to eat, and our impatient drill sergeant was in such a hurry that he ran up to each of us, shouting, "Don't waste time tasting . . . just swallow!"

—NELSON GOULD

Soon after my son, a marine, was deployed to Afghanistan, he called and spent much of the time describing the abject poverty of the people who lived there. When he calmed down, I asked what I thought was a simple question: "What time is it there now?"

That set him off again. "I'm ten and a half hours ahead of you," he replied. "That's how poor this country is. It can't even afford a full time zone."

—ROBIN LYNN MULL

My Afghan interpreter loved using American idioms, even though he rarely had a firm grasp of them. One day, during a meeting with village elders, I asked him to leave out the chitchat and get to the point.

"I understand, sir," he said. "You want me to cut the cheese."

—PATRICK HAWS

During World War II, my friend and I were in a nightclub when two men in uniform asked us to dance. Feeling it was our patriotic duty, we joined them on the dance floor. "So," I asked my partner, "what branch of the service are you in?"

He mumbled, "The Greyhound bus service."

—MARGIE SCHATZ SHEEHAN

My second graders were assigned the task of writing thank-you cards to soldiers serving in the Middle East. One of them wrote, "Thank you for protecting us! I hope we win!"

—GEORGINA MCCARTHY

One of my soldiers in Afghanistan wanted to surprise his wife with flowers for Valentine's Day, but he was afraid she would see the bill before the flowers arrived. So I offered to put the flowers on my credit card and have him pay me in cash. The plan worked beautifully until after Valentine's Day, when my wife received a $120 florist bill but no flowers.

—MICHAEL MERRILL

Ketchikan, Alaska, gets more than 12 feet of rain each year. But the day we visited our grandson Josh, who is stationed at the coast guard base there, the sun decided to shine.

"It's so sunny," I marveled.

"We don't say it's sunny here," corrected Josh. "We refer to it as 'cloud failure.' "

—PATRICIA HARPER

Mail delivery at our base in Japan was irregular at best, so everyone would call the post office to see if the mail had arrived. Tired of the constant calls, the post office manager announced that he would raise a white flag to signal that mail had arrived. That idea was scrapped after soldiers kept calling to ask if the white flag was up.

—DONALD DEREADT

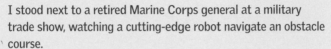

I stood next to a retired Marine Corps general at a military trade show, watching a cutting-edge robot navigate an obstacle course.

"I bet you didn't have these back in your day," I said.

"Oh, we did," he answered. **"They were called privates."**

—CHARLIE BAISLEY

QUOTABLE QUOTES

"I wanted to join the army. The sign said 'Be All That You Can Be.' They told me it wasn't enough."

—JAY LONDON

"I was in the army, and to me it was like a newsreel."

—MEL BROOKS

"Leaders can let you fail and yet not let you be a failure."

—STANLEY MCCHRYSTAL, RETIRED U.S. ARMY FOUR-STAR GENERAL

"Seeing your name on the list for KP or guard duty when you're in the army is like reading a bad review."

—ROBERT DUVALL

"I WAS IN THE ROTC. OF COURSE, ROTC STOOD FOR 'RUNNING OFF TO CANADA.'"

—JAY LENO

"YOU, YOU, AND YOU . . . PANIC. THE REST OF YOU, COME WITH ME."

—U.S. MARINE CORPS GUNNERY SGT.

"Whoever said the pen is mightier than the sword obviously never encountered automatic weapons."

—GEN. DOUGLAS MACARTHUR

"When I lost my rifle, the army charged me $85. That's why in the navy, the captain goes down with the ship."

—COMEDIAN DICK GREGORY

My 11-year-old granddaughter was helping me sort through a pile of papers on my desk. After flipping through page after page of letters from the Department of Veterans Affairs, she turned to me with, I believe, a new appreciation.

"Grandma," she asked, "exactly how many affairs did you have with veterans?"

—SYLVIA FORCE

I was in our local VA hospital when a clerk began scolding a veteran who'd lit up a cigarette in a no-smoking area.

"Sir!" she barked. "When did you start smoking?"

The conversation came to a halt when he replied, "In Vietnam, right after that first bomb dropped."

—DOROTHY KREIPKE-MILLER

My unit was building shelves in the USO at an army camp in Kuwait with the help of a very gruff marine sergeant.

"Sergeant, where do you want this?" I asked, holding up his tape measure.

"Put it with my hat," he said.

"'Hat'? Don't you marines call it a 'cover' or a 'lid'?"

With a look of contempt, he asked, "Do I look like a Crock-Pot to you?"

—BONAH BACHENHEIMER

After my husband, a veteran, spoke at an elementary school, a student asked what he ate during battle.

"C rations," he replied.

"Ooh!" she squealed. "I love seafood."

—DOTTY BOEZINGER

Lt. Gen. William "Gus" Pagonis told the story of going to a movie shortly after retiring. When he and his wife walked into the near-empty theater, a young man stood up and pointed at them. Used to the attention, General Pagonis launched into a speech, thanking the young man and saying how pleased he and his wife were to be there and how—

"Uhh . . ." interrupted the confused usher. "I'm just counting customers. We need ten people before they can start the film."

—TERRI KOYL

Upon returning from a stint in Iraq, my sister insisted that the best part about being home was having real food again: "The Lunchables I had for breakfast was great!"

—GARRETT LEE THORNE

After 29 years of military service, I figured some of my interest in military history would have rubbed off on my 14-year-old son. Wrong! While helping him prepare for his Civil War exam, I asked, "Why did General Lee take his army north to Gettysburg?"

His response: "To listen to Lincoln's speech."

—DONNA WILLIAMS

It was the '60s, and our unit command decided to let us have mustaches, something our first sergeant clearly opposed. Nevertheless, he told us to go ahead and grow one. A week later, he appeared before the morning formation with a razor. He proceeded to shave off each of our mustaches and let the hairs fall into individual envelopes on which he wrote our name. "Now," he announced, "if anyone asks where your mustache is, tell him it's in the sergeant's safe."

—GARY MUFFITT

At a formal NATO dinner, a British officer commented on my ceremonial spurs. "Wearing them is a tradition for U.S. Cavalry officers," I explained.

He smiled with more than a bit of condescension. "My dear boy, the United States Army doesn't have traditions. It has habits."

—STEVEN EDEN

Base rules required that everything around the aircraft hangar at our air force base be painted a bright yellow. When our sergeant noticed that the newly issued trash cans were not yellow, he snarled to an airman, "When I come back tomorrow, I better not see those trash cans unpainted." He got his wish. The next morning, all the new trash cans were gone.

—JOHN LEARD

While serving in Vietnam, I met some camouflaged soldiers sitting in a converted fishing boat that had a camouflaged engine and machine gun.

"Great camo job," I told them. "No one will ever spot you."

"There's one slight flaw," one of the soldiers said, lifting up a life vest. "We're required to wear these bright orange life preservers when under way."

—WILLIAM KAY

Eggs in the military rarely come from chickens. Instead, they're hatched in powder form. As I prepared to make scrambled eggs during KP duty, I filled a large tub with water and poured in a 25-pound bag of the stuff. As I stirred, my mess sergeant threw four whole eggs in, shells and all.

"Why'd you do that?" I asked.

His reply: "So when they bite into a shell, they'll think it's real."

—JASON MICKOLIO

"Look at it this way:
Most people have to pay to go on a cruise."

My father served in the Seabees, which meant he was more likely to handle a cement mixer than a rifle. I tried to explain this to my six-year-old son.

"Grandpa didn't fight in any battles," I said. "He wasn't that kind of soldier."

"Oh," said my son. "He was in the Salvation Army."

—JODI WEBB

A woman called our restaurant. "I want to treat my husband to breakfast for Veteran's Day," she said. "Do you still offer free meals to veterans?"

—JOHN BARTUSKA

When I was stationed in Naples with the U.S. Navy, my wife and I became parents of a baby girl, the first grandchild on both sides of the family. Soon after, my in-laws were out to dinner with another couple who were also new grandparents. My mother-in-law listened patiently as the other woman detailed what a joy it was babysitting for her new granddaughter. Not to be outdone, my mother-in-law said, "Well, my granddaughter is touring Europe."

—MARK NOVAK

Discussing phone etiquette for naval recruits, our lieutenant recalled a cautionary tale about the time he thought he was calling the ship's chart house.

A sleepy voice answered, "Yeah, whaddaya want?"

"That's no way to answer a phone when an officer calls," he snarled. "Now let's start over. Pretend I just called you."

"Okay. Captain's cabin, captain speaking!"

—HERM ALBRIGHT

When I was a convoy commander in Iraq, my radio call signal was Rolling Thunder Five. Eventually, I shortened it and would just state, "This is Thunder Five. Over." But I went back to using my full call sign a few days later after an honest sergeant clued me in to something.

"You know, ma'am," he said, "it sounds like you're saying, 'This is Thunder Thighs' over the radio."

—LEANNE D. WELDIN

A truck we were towing back to Rhein-Main Air Base in Germany crashed, and the senior airman had to fill out an accident report, per regulations. He began, "In the process of towing, we heard a loud noise in the rear. I became concerned when the vehicle in tow passed me with no driver in it."

—GEORGE DESPIRITO

Comedian Paul Gilmartin has trouble imagining what our soldiers have to deal with in Afghanistan: "Desert combat? I can't even stand the walk back from the beach to the car."

Due to a manpower shortage at our air force base in England, the commander nixed all afternoons off. That same day, an airman broached the subject with him.

"Didn't you hear what I said this morning?" our commander snapped. "You'd better have a great reason."

"Sir," said the airman, "my wife is expecting to get pregnant this afternoon, and I want to be there when it happens."

He got the afternoon off.

—PAT FERRY

It was nighttime in Vietnam. All was quiet in our forward outpost when a perimeter guard opened up with grenades and automatic rifle fire. It sounded like all of North Vietnam was attacking. I sprinted over to him.

"What is it?!" I hollered.

The pandemonium stilled, and a small, frightened voice replied, **"Big snake, sir."**

—CRAIG MACNAB

Pulling guard duty is dull work. But I never realized just how dull until one night when, with nothing else to do, I looked underneath my desk. There I found these words scrawled by a predecessor: "Man, you must really be bored!"

—MICHAEL BIELARSKI

When my ex-marine father-in-law was at my house, our six-year-old neighbor came by to play with my kids.

I asked her if she knew who he was. She looked up at him with her big blue eyes and said, "I don't remember what his name is, but I know he used to be a submarine."

—JANELLE RAGLAND

After serving 11 years in the navy, I was discharged with—shall we say—a vastly increased vocabulary. This became evident one day as I drove with my five-year-old daughter. Everyone on the road was annoying me, and I let each of them know it.

Eventually, my daughter asked, "Daddy, why are all the bad drivers around you and not Mommy?"

—JOHN ERNEST SWAPP

A general walked into an elevator on base that was occupied by a specialist. "What are you doing to prepare for your deployment to Afghanistan, Specialist?" he asked.

Flustered, the specialist simply shrugged.

This didn't sit well with the general. He went to the officer in charge and demanded to know why his soldiers seemed unprepared. The officer assembled his staff in an attempt to figure out the problem, and soon we all received this memo: "As of today, specialists are no longer allowed to take the elevator."

—LT. GALEN P. MAHON

LAST LAUGHS

We were headed to a resort when my father got hopelessly lost. Spotting a farmer in his field, Dad pulled over and asked for directions to Lake Ronkonkoma.

"Never heard of it," said the farmer. "But you're going the wrong way."

—NICK DEMARTINO

Shopping in a supermarket, my friend spotted a pregnant woman who looked ready to give birth. She ran to the manager's office and screamed, "Do something! Her water's broken! I can see water at her feet!"

Returning a week later, she bumped into the manager. "So did the woman give birth?" she asked.

"Yes," he replied. "To a large frozen chicken that was hidden up her shirt."

—BRENDA BRENNAN

I want to take one of those English as a Second Language courses—just go in and blow everybody away on the first day.

—COMEDIAN CRAIG ANTON

The plan: to build a garden walkway made up of dozens of wooden squares. I decided I'd slice railroad ties into two-inch thick pieces for the sections. That's what I told the clerk at the lumber yard.

"You got a power saw?" he asked.

"No," I said. "Can't I just use my hand saw?"

He nodded slowly. "You could. But I just have one question. How old do you want to be when you finish?"

—JUDY MYERS

"Are you the one who called about the leaky faucet?"

My father is a glass-half-empty-and-probably-polluted kind of guy. So during a trip to the zoo, I wasn't surprised by his reaction when a magnificent peacock strutted past. As my family admired the polychromatic feathers, Dad wondered, "Can you imagine what that thing would look like without feathers?"

—CHRIS LOUGHRAN

Finding a bottle on the beach, Jake uncorks it and releases a genie. "Ah, now you get three wishes," says the genie.

"Great!" Jake replies. "First, I want one billion dollars." Poof! There's a flash, and a paper with Swiss bank account numbers appears in Jake's hand.

"Next, I want a Ferrari." Poof! Another flash, and a shiny red Ferrari is parked next to him.

"Finally," Jake says, "I want to be irresistible to women." Poof! There's another blinding flash, and Jake turns into a box of chocolates.

—RICHARD A. WRIGHT

While we were visiting Block Island, off the New England coast, my friend, who'd had a few, called to ask me for a ride home. "I'm outside Iggi's Inn," he slurred.

After many hours—and even more miles—driving around looking for Iggi's Inn, I finally found him. He was leaning against a large sign for the 1661 Inn.

—CLAYTON LUCE

As I shopped, the following announcement came over the department store's PA system: "If someone here has a convertible with the top down, it just started raining. Towels are located in aisle five."

—SHERRY BAILEY

As I stepped out of the shower, I heard someone in my kitchen downstairs. Knowing that my wife was out, I grabbed my 1903 heirloom rifle—which no longer works—and crept downstairs, forgetting the fact that I was in my birthday suit.

I came around the corner with the gun raised, only to find my wife loading the dishwasher.

"What are you doing?" she asked.

"I thought I heard an intruder. I came down to scare him."

Scanning the contours of my doughy, naked body, she mumbled, "You didn't need the gun."

—KURT EPPS

Working on a new trick, a magician turned his wife into a couch and his kids into chairs, but he couldn't turn them back. What have I done? he wondered. How can I bring back my family? Out of ideas, he loaded everybody into his van and rushed to the hospital. He explained the situation, and his family was whisked off to surgery. Hours later, the surgeon emerged.

"How are they?" the magician asked.

"Comfortable."

—BOB MEYERSON

I entered an auction at an out-of-town convention and won a large Queen Anne wingback chair. Getting it back to my seventh-floor hotel room proved a challenge. I got it in the elevator, but there wasn't enough room for everyone, so I invited another woman to take a seat. We stopped on the third floor, and a drunk started to enter. He looked at the woman on the chair for a second before suggesting, **"If I were you, I'd ask for a bigger room."**

—THAYER DONOVAN

My husband and I love that nearly every flashing construction sign we pass has some sort of typo. Our favorite: "Caution! Loose Gravey Ahead!"

—TERRA COSTIN

I was at the drugstore and noticed a young male cashier staring at the pretty girl in front of me. Her total came to $14.62, and after handing over a $100 bill, she waited for change. "Here you go," said the cashier, smiling as he returned the proper amount. "Have a great day!"

Now I placed my items on the counter. The tally was $32.79, and I, too, gave the cashier a $100 bill. "I'm sorry, ma'am. We can't accept anything larger than a fifty," he told me, pointing to a sign stating store policy.

"But you just accepted that last girl's hundred," I reasoned.

"I had to," he said. "It had her phone number on it."

—KAREN REHM

In ancient Greece, a man came running up to Socrates with gossip he'd heard about Diogenes.

"Before you tell me," interrupted Socrates, "are you sure that what you are about to tell me is true?"

"No," admitted the man.

"Is what you are about to tell me about Diogenes something good?"

"No, but he . . ."

"Will this news benefit me?"

"No, but Diogenes . . ."

"If what you want to tell me is not true, not good, and of no benefit, why tell it to me at all?"

The man walked away in shame. And that's how Socrates never found out that Diogenes was fooling around with his wife.

QUOTABLE QUOTES

"I'VE NEVER BEEN SWIMMING. THAT'S BECAUSE IT'S NEVER BEEN MORE THAN HALF AN HOUR SINCE I LAST ATE."

—COMEDIAN ARTIE LANGE

"I never sing in the shower. It's very dangerous."

—JIMMY FALLON

"Three groups spend other people's money: children, thieves, politicians. All three need supervision."

—DICK ARMEY

"I BELIEVE IN LOOKING REALITY STRAIGHT IN THE EYE AND DENYING IT."

—GARRISON KEILLOR

"A person without a sense of humor is like a wagon without springs. It's jolted by every pebble on the road."

—HENRY WARD BEECHER

"THE TROUBLE WITH JOGGING IS THAT THE ICE FALLS OUT OF YOUR GLASS."

—MARTIN MULL

"Always buy a good bed and a good pair of shoes. If you're not in one, you're in the other."

—GLORIA HUNNIFORD

"Just dialed the wrong person on Skype. Guess I made a Skypo."

—ALLEN KLEIN

"My grandmother started walking five miles a day when she was sixty. She's ninety-seven now, and we don't know where the hell she is."

—ELLEN DEGENERES

Every year on my birthday, I looked forward to my aunt's gift—a scarf, hat or sweater knitted by hand. One year, she must have had better things to do because I received a ball of yarn, knitting needles and a how-to-knit book. Her card read **"Scarf, some assembly required."**

—DIONNE OBESO

An 80-year-old man goes to a doctor for a checkup. The doctor is amazed at his shape. "To what do you attribute your good health?"

"I'm a turkey hunter, and that's why I'm in good shape. Get up before daylight, chase turkeys up and down mountains."

The doctor says, "Well, I'm sure it helps, but there have to be genetic factors. How old was your dad when he died?"

"Who says my dad's dead?"

"You're 80 years old and your dad's alive? How old is he?"

"Dad's 100. In fact, he turkey hunted with me this morning."

"What about your dad's dad—how old was he when he died?"

"Who says my grandpa's dead?"

"You're 80 years old and your grandfather's still living? How old is he?"

"Grandpa's 118."

"I suppose you're going to tell me he went turkey hunting this morning?"

"No. He got married."

The doctor looks at the man in amazement. "Got married? Why would a 118-year-old guy want to get married?"

The old-timer answers, "Who says he wanted to?"

—ARDELL WIECZOREK

A hunter sneaked up on a duck and was about to fire when the duck yelled, "Don't shoot, and I'll give you a hot stock tip!"

"Okay," the hunter replied. "What's the stock?"

"It's a company called Sounds Like a Duck," the fowl said. "It manufactures a duck call, and the share price went up two points last week."

The hunter immediately went home and bought a thousand shares, figuring if anyone could determine an effective duck call it would be a duck. But just two weeks later, the company went out of business. Furious, the hunter drove back to the pond to get an explanation.

"I just lost thousands of dollars because of your lousy tip," the hunter said angrily.

"Big deal," the duck replied. "We just lost our early warning system."

—DONALD F. NIGRONI

With a new book on handwriting analysis, I began practicing on colleagues at work. One skeptical woman asked if she could bring in a sample of her daughter's writing. "Of course," I replied.

Next day, the woman handed me an envelope. I opened it, read the contents, then dramatically told her, "Your daughter is 14 years old. She's an A student. She loves music and horses."

Amazed, the woman ran off to tell her friends before I could show her the note. It read: "I'm 14 years old and an A student. I love music and horses. My mother thinks you're a fake."

—BILL WHITMAN

What do you get if you divide the circumference of your jack-o'-lantern by its diameter?
Pumpkin pi.

BEN ARNOLD-BIK

On our first visit together to a nearby amusement park, my husband immediately fell in love with a big, colorful Dr. Seuss hat he saw many people wearing. Soon we found out that the hats were given away to winners at one of the park's more difficult arcade games. That day, and on each of our following four trips to the park, we spent ridiculous amounts of money trying to win the hat but never succeeded.

On our fifth visit, our friend Gerard came with us. When told of our frustrating hat saga, he said, "No problem. Give me a few minutes, and I'll get one."

My husband and I snickered to ourselves as Gerard left. But sure enough, just a few minutes later, he was back with the beloved hat in hand. "I can't believe it," my husband said as he triumphantly placed the hat atop his head. "Have you played that game before?"

"What game?" Gerard replied. "I bought the hat at the souvenir store."

—MARLA SARINO

While sightseeing at George Washington's home in Mount Vernon, Virginia, a family friend became nervous when she thought she had lost two of my cousins. She looked everywhere and called out their names repeatedly. Soon our friend grew perturbed that not one of the Mount Vernon employees had joined in the search. Instead, they simply stood around, staring at her as if she were crazy. Finally, just a few moments later, my cousins—George and Martha—came out from hiding.

—TRACY NELSON

Sign spotted on a telephone pole in my neighborhood:
"Garage Sale this Saturday—7 a.m. until 100 degrees."

—KATHY RICHEY

"I took the road less traveled."

A pig walks into a bar, orders 15 beers and knocks them back. "You've had a lot to drink. Would you like to know where the bathroom is?" asks the bartender.

"No," says the hog. "I'm the little pig that goes wee-wee-wee all the way home."

**A man noted for his tact was awakened one morning at four o'clock by his ringing telephone.
"Your dog's barking and it's keeping me awake," said an irate voice.
The man thanked the caller and politely asked his name before hanging up. The next morning at four o'clock, he called back his neighbor.**

"Sir," he said, "I don't have a dog."

—RUTH MEYERS

The last thing my friend Christy was prepared for was an invitation to a costume party. Eight and a half months pregnant, she was in no shape for any conventional costume. Still, she wanted to go, so she painted a big yellow circle on an extra-extra large white T-shirt, dug a pair of red devil horns out of her kids' Halloween junk pile . . . and went as a deviled egg.

—BETTY C. HATCHER

Being Korean, I asked my Tennessean friend, "What's the difference between whiskey and moonshine?"

His reply: "Tax."

—KISU KIM

Bored during a long flight, an eminent scholar leaned over and woke up the sleeping man next to him to ask if he would like to play a game. "I'll ask you a question," the scholar explained, "and if you don't know the answer, you pay me $5. Then you ask me a question, and if I don't know the answer, I'll pay you $50."

When the man agreed to play, the scholar asked, "What's the distance from the earth to the moon?"

Flummoxed, the man handed him $5. "Ha!" said the scholar. "It's 238,857 miles. Now it's your turn."

The man was silent for a few moments. Then he asked, "What goes up a hill with three legs and comes down with four?"

Puzzled, the scholar racked his brains for an hour—but to no avail. Finally, he took out his wallet and handed over $50. "Okay, what is the answer?" the scholar asked.

The man said, "I don't know," pulled out a $5 bill, handed it to the scholar and went back to sleep.

—KRIS UEBERRHEIN

My husband, who uses a wheelchair, showed up at his eye doctor's for an appointment. The receptionist checked the schedule, then said, "The nurse will call you in a moment. Have a seat."

He smiled. "Done."

—KIM FRIEDMAN

I never realized just how small my grandparents' town was until we decided to see a movie on Main Street. We called the theater and asked what time the film started. The manager replied, **"When can you get here?"**

—ELISE JONES

About an hour after our son Noah was born, and while my parents were getting acquainted with him, our minister stopped in to visit. Noah, who had been quiet until then, cried as soon as the pastor spoke.

"That's odd," the pastor said, "he should be used to my voice. He's been hearing my sermons for nine months."

"Yes," Dad retorted, "but this is the first chance he's had to comment on them."

—TARA RUEL

Late one night, Norm's doorbell rang. When he answered the door, he found a six-foot cockroach standing there. The bug grabbed Norm by the collar, punched him in the eye, threw him across the living room and then ran off.

The next day, Norm went to see his doctor to have his bruised eye examined.

"Ah, yes," the doctor said when Norm explained what had happened.

"There's a nasty bug going around."

—DONALD GEISER

Revenge of the blondes . . .

Q: Why are so many blonde jokes one-liners?
A: So brunettes can remember them.

Q: What do brunettes miss most about a great party?
A: The invitation.

Q: What do you call a good-looking man with a brunette?
A: A hostage.

Q: What's black and blue and brown and lying in a ditch?
A: A brunette who has told too many blonde jokes.

"You've gotta help me," the man said to the psychiatrist. "Every night this week I've dreamed I'm playing in a badminton tournament. Then I wake up tired and sweaty."

"Okay, here's your medicine," the doctor said. "Drink this right away, and you'll be cured in no time.

"Can't I wait and drink it tomorrow?" the dreamer wanted to know.

"Why?" the doctor asked.

"It's our championship game tonight."

—EMILY LEYBLE

Recently, my girlfriend, Karen, got a job at a local hardware store. "The owners don't want us hanging out with our friends," she said. "If you stop by, tell them you're my brother."

On my first visit, I walked to the customer service desk and asked the older woman there, "Is Karen around?" When she looked at me quizzically, I added, "I'm her brother."

She smiled. "What a nice surprise. I'm Karen's mother."

—ANAND MAHARAJ

During a state visit to Great Britain, President Ronald Reagan purportedly went horseback riding with Queen Elizabeth. At one point, one of the horses passed gas quite loudly. The queen apologized, saying, "There are some things even royalty can't control."

Reagan replied, "I'm glad you told me, or I would have thought it was the horse."

The new phone book arrived with a handy blank emergency-number form attached to the front page. I guess everyone's notion of an emergency is different. The categories for phone numbers were listed in this order: 1. Pizza 2. Takeout Restaurants 3. Taxi 4. Poison Control 5. Doctor.

—MEGHAN HUNSAKER

As I helped my elderly neighbor clean out his garage, I stumbled upon an ax in the corner.

"That was my grandfather's," he said, picking it up and running his fingers along the blade. **"Of course, it's been through three new heads since he last used it."**

—BEN KREUSSER

? **Why did the new race-car driver make so many stops?**

Because some guy on the side of the road kept flagging him down.

— STEVE JOHNSON

One afternoon I rushed out of the house, forgetting my keys, and found myself locked out. There was nothing I could do but wait for my husband to come home, so I went over to a neighbor who was outside raking leaves.

"You locked yourself out?" he said.

"Yeah. This is the second time since we moved in. After the first time we took an extra key and put it in a jar, then stuck it in a potted plant on the back deck."

"So what's the problem?"

"I took the plants in for the winter."

—ADRIANA DESIMONE

A man walked into his backyard one morning and found a gorilla in a tree. He called a gorilla-removal service, and soon a serviceman arrived with a stick, a Chihuahua, a pair of handcuffs and a shotgun.

"Now listen carefully," he told the homeowner. "I'm going to climb the tree and poke the gorilla with this stick until he falls to the ground. The trained Chihuahua will then go right for his, uh, sensitive area, and when the gorilla instinctively crosses his hands in front to protect himself, you slap on the handcuffs."

"Got it," the homeowner replied. "But what's the shotgun for?"

"If I fall out of the tree before the gorilla," the man said, "shoot the Chihuahua."

—TIMOTHY SLEDGE

One would be hard-pressed to pass on this ad, spotted on Craigslist: "1990 Ford Escort $250. Could be driven. Should be towed."

—RYAN MALLOY

Apparently I tend to brag too much about my home state of Ohio. One day I told a long-suffering friend, "You know, the first man in powered flight was from Ohio. The first man to orbit the earth was from Ohio. And the first man on the moon was from Ohio."

"Sounds like a lot of people are trying to get out of Ohio."

—JEAN NEIDHARDT

Feeling sick, my sister grabbed the thermometer from the medicine cabinet and popped it into her mouth.

"Uh, Julie, that's the dog's thermometer," said my mother.

Julie spit out the thermometer. "Ewww, that was in Fitzie's mouth?!"

Mom hesitated before replying, "Not exactly."

—JANET GALLO

After my parents passed away, my wife and I transferred thousands of their 35-mm slides to videotape, using freezer bags to organize the project. After the videotape was complete, my stepdaughter came for a visit and did a double take when she noticed a bag of turkey meat that my wife was defrosting on the counter. It was labeled "Dave's Folks."

—DAVID HYRE

To me, boxing is like ballet, except there's no music and no choreography, and the dancers hit each other.

—JACK HANDEY

I'm a stickler about people spelling my first name correctly: K-A-T-H-Y. One day, I went to an electronics store where they ask for your name when you buy something. I told the clerk my name is Kathy with a K. He didn't say anything as I paid for my goods and left the store. Later, when I looked at my receipt, I saw that he had noted my name: Cathy Withakay.

—KATHY LANDERKIN

"Every year I say, 'Just a little off the top,' but they never listen!"

During a game of Scrabble, my aunt decided to pass. "I simply can't move my vowels," she complained.

My uncle replied, **"Does that mean you're consonated?"**

—SUZANNE CARLSON

I just watched my dog chase his tail for ten minutes, and I thought to myself, *Wow, dogs are easily entertained.* Then I realized: I just watched my dog chase his tail for ten minutes.

—ADAM JOSHUA SMARGON

Since I was a new patient, I had to fill out an information form for the doctor's files. The nurse reading it over noticed my unusual name.

"How do you pronounce it?" she asked.

"Na-le-Y-ko," I said, proud of my Ukranian heritage.

"That sounds real nice," she said, smiling.

"Yes, it is melodious," I agreed.

"So," she asked sweetly, "what part of Melodia is your family from?"

—ANN NALYWAJKO

In an attempt to balance work and motherhood, I delegated the grocery shopping to my young babysitter. But the job proved a tad daunting. One day while I was at work, she texted me from the supermarket.

"Can't find Brillo pads," she wrote. "All they have are Tampax and Kotex."

—KIMBERLY CLARK

Vacationing in Hawaii, two priests decide to wear casual clothes so they won't be identified as clergy. They buy Hawaiian shirts and sandals and soon hit the beach. They notice a gorgeous blonde in a tiny bikini.

"Good afternoon, Fathers," she says as she strolls by.

The men are stunned. How does she know they're clergy? Later they buy even wilder attire: surfer shorts, tie-dyed T-shirts and dark glasses.

The next day, they return to the beach. The same fabulous blonde, now wearing a string bikini, passes by, nods politely at them and says, "Good morning, Fathers."

"Just a minute, young lady," says one of the priests. "We are priests and proud of it, but how in the world did you know?"

"Don't you recognize me? I'm Sister Kathryn from the convent."

—MICHAEL RANA

After she fainted, my mother was raced to the hospital. Her doctor asked, "Why do you think you passed out?" Looking at him oddly, Mom replied,

"Because I woke up on the floor."

—JEFFREY WARD

My mother enjoys shopping at those dollar stores where almost everything costs just a buck. Recently Mom commented to a cashier that she loves shopping at the store when she is depressed because you can buy so much for so little. When the cashier rang up her purchases and the total came to $99.58, a woman behind her quipped, "You must have been on the verge of suicide!"

—DAVID SINGH

"Looks like somebody's using your Rogaine."

A friend of mine had been wanting new kitchen cabinets for a long time, but her husband insisted they were an extravagance. She went to visit her mother for two weeks, and when she returned, she was overjoyed to find that beautiful new cabinets had been installed.

A few days later, a neighbor came over to visit my friend. After admiring the new cabinets, the neighbor added, "All of us were so glad that the fire your husband had while you were gone was confined to the kitchen."

—MARGARET GUNN

Two great white sharks swimming in the ocean spy some surfers. The younger one licks his lips and makes a beeline for them.

"Just a minute," says his father, stopping him. "First we swim around them with just the tip of our fins showing."

And they do.

"Now we swim around them a few times with all our fins showing."

And they do.

"Now we eat everybody."

When they are both gorged, the son asks, "Dad, why didn't we just eat them when we first saw them?"

"Because they taste better without all the poop inside."

—FRANK JOHNSTON

Eight and a half months very pregnant with twins, I was used to getting nervous glances from strangers. But I never realized how imposing I was until my husband and I went out to dinner at a new restaurant. The hostess sat us at our table, took a long look at my stomach and asked, "Would you like me to get you a high chair just in case?"

—CARISSA LUCYK

My friend's ad: "For Sale: '96 Mitsubishi Eclipse Spyder. Brand-new convertible top and tires. Needs minor work. Serious injuries only!"

—DR. NAVJOT GILL

I recently visited my son while he was doing some remodeling at his house. As he left one morning, he told me I'd need to let the plumber in to do some work in the bathroom. Thinking I wouldn't want to let just anyone into the house, I asked how I could recognize him.

Without missing a beat, my son replied, "He'll be carrying a toilet."

—AVA C. SHAUGHNESSY

The local wholesale warehouse sells everything from tires to tuna fish. I was there around noon and stopped at the lunch counter for a slice of pizza. I ate only half of it and threw my leftovers in a nearby trash can.

Then I turned to see a man standing there, hot dog in one hand, ketchup in the other, with a look of horror on his face. I asked him what was wrong. He said, "I just purchased that trash can!"

—CHRIS BIRCH

Sometimes I'll stand up in a meeting and say, "You just gave me an idea!" Then I leave the room, drive home and go to bed.

—TIM SIEDELL

What does it mean when you find a bear with a wet nose?

It means you're too close to the bear.

DAVID GAY

The topic of conversation at our neighbors' barbecue was their beautiful new lawn. It especially sparkled next to the dying brown patch of earth on our side of the fence. My husband, Bob, had a ready excuse.

"Look at what our gardener did!" he said. **"He put the sod in upside down."**

—PAMELA WIEBUSCH

After one of my students acted up, I took him to our school psychiatrist, who asked if he had ADHD.

"No," said the boy. "I just have a normal TV."

—MATTHEW HUGHES

One weekend, a doctor, a priest and an attorney were out in a fishing boat. Their motor had conked out and one of the oars had drifted off. Just as the doctor was about to dive in to retrieve the oar, the boat was surrounded by sharks.

"I can't go now," the doctor said. "If someone gets bitten, you'll need my services."

"I can't go either," said the priest. "If the doctor fails, I'll need to give last rites."

"Fine," said the attorney. "I'll get it." He dove in, the sharks moved, he retrieved the oar and climbed back into the boat. The doctor and priest looked flabbergasted. The attorney just smiled and said, "Professional courtesy."

—MELODY LEE

Also Available
from Reader's Digest

Laughter, the Best Medicine

More than 600 jokes, gags, and laugh lines. Drawn from one of the most popular features of *Reader's Digest* magazine, this lighthearted collection of jokes, one-liners, and other glimpses of life is just what the doctor ordered.

ISBN 978-0-89577-977-9 • $9.95 paperback

Laughter Really Is the Best Medicine

Guaranteed to put laughter in your day, this side-splitting compilation of jokes pokes fun at the facts and foibles of daily routines.This little volume is sure to tickle your funny bone.

ISBN 978-1-60652-204-2 • $9.95 paperback

Humor In Uniform

This laugh-out-loud collection includes 400 of the funniest jokes, quotes, and cartoons from the well-know column in *Reader's Digest* magazine. Enjoy these anecdotes, all supplied by those in the U.S. military and their families.

ISBN 978-0-7621-0929-6 • $9.99 paperback

For more information, visit us at RDTradePublishing.com
E-book editions are also available.

Reader's Digest books can be purchased through
retail and online bookstores.